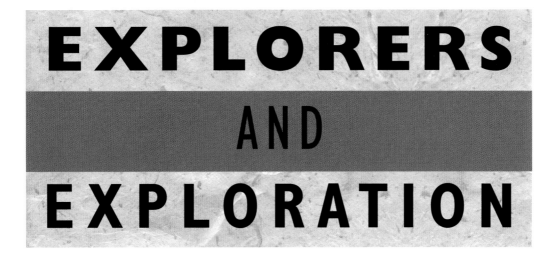

EXPLORERS
AND
EXPLORATION

10

SUBMERSIBLES – ZHANG QIAN

Marshall Cavendish
New York • London • Singapore

Marshall Cavendish
99 White Plains Road
Tarrytown, New York 10591-9001

www.marshallcavendish.com

Consultants: Ralph Ehrenberg, former chief, Geography and Map Division, Library of Congress, Washington, DC; Conrad Heidenreich, former historical geography professor, York University, Toronto; Shane Winser, information officer, Royal Geographical Society, London

Contributing authors: Dale Anderson, Kay Barnham, Peter Chrisp, Richard Dargie, Paul Dowswell, Elizabeth Gogerly, Steven Maddocks, John Malam, Stewart Ross, Shane Winser

MARSHALL CAVENDISH
Editor: Thomas McCarthy
Editorial Director: Paul Bernabeo
Production Manager: Michael Esposito

WHITE-THOMSON PUBLISHING
Editors: Alex Woolf and Steven Maddocks
Design: Ross George and Derek Lee
Cartographer: Peter Bull Design
Picture Research: Glass Onion Pictures
Indexer: Fiona Barr

ISBN 0-7614-7535-4 (set)
ISBN 0-7614-7545-1 (vol. 10)

Printed in China

08 07 06 05 04   5 4 3 2 1

Library of Congress Cataloging-in-Publication Data
Explorers and exploration.
    p. cm.
  Includes bibliographical references (p.   ) and index.
  ISBN 0-7614-7535-4 (set : alk. paper) -- ISBN 0-7614-7536-2 (v. 1) -- ISBN 0-7614-7537-0 (v. 2) -- ISBN 0-7614-7538-9 (v. 3) -- ISBN 0-7614-7539-7 (v. 4) -- ISBN 0-7614-7540-0 (v. 5) -- ISBN 0-7614-7541-9 (v. 6) -- ISBN 0-7614-7542-7 (v. 7) -- ISBN 0-7614-7543-5 (v. 8) -- ISBN 0-7614-7544-3 (v. 9) -- ISBN 0-7614-7545-1 (v. 10) -- ISBN 0-7614-7546-X (v. 11)
  1. Explorers--Encyclopedias. 2. Discoveries in geography--Encyclopedias. I. Marshall Cavendish Corporation. II. Title.
  G80.E95 2005
  910'.92'2--dc22

                    2004048292

ILLUSTRATION CREDITS
Art Archive: 798.

AKG London: 729, 736, 744, 745, 746, 747, 757, 766, 769, 772, 782, 783, 786, 787, 789.

Bridgeman Art Library: 730 (Giraudon), 732, 737, 738, 748 (Giraudon), 750 (Walters Art Museum, Baltimore, MD), 751 (The Stapleton Collection), 754, 765 (New York Historical Society), 770 (Archives Charmet), 778 (Royal Geographical Society, London), 780, 788 (Archives Charmet), 796 (Paul Freeman).

NASA: 781, 784.

Royal Geographical Society, London: 728, 731, 733, 735, 755, 777, 790, 791, 794, 795.

Science Photo Library: 724 (Alexis Rosenfeld), 727 (Dr. Ken Macdonald), 742 (NASA), 752 (David Nunuk), 758 (Volker Steger).

Topham Picturepoint: 725, 726, 739, 740 (British Museum, London / HIP), 741 (Science Museum, London / HIP), 756, 759, 760, 761, 762, 764, 773 (Image Works), 774 (British Library, London / HIP), 776, 792, 793.

Cover: Tide predictor, 1580 (Topham Picturepoint / British Museum, London / HIP).

color key	time period
▬▬▬	to 500
▬▬▬	500–1400
▬▬▬	1400–1850
▬▬▬	1850–1945
▬▬▬	1945–2000
▬▬▬	general articles

CONTENTS

SUBMERSIBLES

FIRST DEVELOPED DURING THE 1960s, submersibles are vehicles used for underwater exploration. In a submersible a scientist is able to travel to depths that would normally be out of reach to humans. In the deep oceans in conditions utterly unlike those that support life on the earth's surface, remarkable new ecosystems are being discovered. Submersibles are also used by underwater archaeologists searching for sunken ships and by engineers for the construction and maintenance of oil pipelines and other underwater structures.

Right **The *Nautile,* a titanium-hulled French minisubmarine equipped with cameras, lights, and robotic arms, can spend up to five hours underwater at depths up to 20,000 feet (6.1 km). *Nautile* is best known for its investigation of the wreck of the *Titanic,* located on the floor of the Atlantic, 12,500 feet (3.81 km) down.**

BATHYSPHERE

In the early 1930s William Beebe (1877–1962), an American biologist frustrated by the limitations of his hard-helmet diving suit, together with his partner Otis Barton, built an underwater observation chamber called a bathysphere. A steel sphere less than 5 feet (1.5 m) in diameter, the bathysphere had walls 1.6 inches (4 cm) thick, with three portholes made of quartz (a hard, colorless mineral). On August 15, 1934, on a ship off the coast of Bermuda, the two explorers climbed inside the bathysphere. The door was closed with ten massive bolts, and the 4,500-pound (2,041 kg) vessel was lowered by a ship's winch suspended from a steel cable to a record-breaking depth of 3,031 feet (924 m). Upon returning to the surface, the men reported that below a depth of 1,000 feet (305 m) was total darkness, with occasional flashes of light emitted by odd-looking fish.

BATHYSCAPHE

Beebe's bathysphere was dependent on its support ship and could travel only up and down its steel cable. After World War II the

Above **William Beebe, the inventor of the bathysphere, photographed in 1930.**

Swiss physicist Auguste Piccard, who had pioneered high-altitude balloon flights, began testing an untethered underwater research vessel, which he called a bathyscaphe.

The descent of Piccard's bathyscaphe was controlled by a combination of ballast (materials that make a vessel heavier or lighter) and a huge tank filled with gasoline. Since gasoline is lighter than water, the vessel was naturally buoyant. To begin the descent, air was released from ballast tanks and replaced by water to make the vessel heavy. As the bathyscaphe descended, the increasing water pressure gradually compressed the gasoline and thus reduced the vessel's buoyancy and speeded up its descent. To slow down the descent or to begin ascending, lead ballast was released to make the vessel lighter.

On January 23, 1960, Auguste's son Jacques Piccard, together with Don Walsh of the U.S. Navy, made a dive in a bathyscaphe called *Trieste*. The two men reached the deepest place on earth, the Marianas Trench, 35,830 feet (10,916 m) beneath the Pacific Ocean. In the beam of their searchlights, they saw a flat fish with bulging eyes, their observation providing the first conclusive evidence that life exists in the deepest oceans. The journey of the *Trieste* took eight and a half hours. Piccard and Walsh are still the only people to have traveled to such a depth.

William Beebe had the impression of entering a new world when he was lowered into the depths of the Atlantic Ocean:

As I peered down I realised I was looking towards a world of life almost as unknown as that of Mars or Venus. A world in which, up to the present time, our efforts at capturing the inhabitants have been pitifully trivial. Modern oceanographic knowledge of deep sea fish is comparable to the information of a student of African mammals, who has trapped a small collection of rats and mice but is still wholly unaware of antelope, elephants, lions, and rhinos.

William Beebe, *Half Mile Down* (1934)

Trieste had the disadvantage of not being particularly easy to maneuver. In 1964 the U.S. Navy established the Woods Hole Oceanographic Institution (WHOI) at Cape Cod, Massachusetts, with the purpose of building a small, more maneuverable manned submersible, which was given the name *Alvin*. Still in use, *Alvin* has undergone a great many improvements and modifications during its lifetime and contributed to some of the greatest deep-sea discoveries of the twentieth century.

UNMANNED SUBMERSIBLES

Since many underwater areas are too dangerous to be investigated at close quarters by manned submersibles, scientists wanting to explore such areas must use unmanned robotic submersibles instead. In 1986, during his exploration of the wreck of HMS *Titanic*, the American marine archaeologist Robert Ballard tested a small remotely operated vehicle (ROV) called *Jason Junior*, or *JJ*. The ROV was attached by cables to *Alvin*, from where Ballard controlled its movements.

1934
William Beebe's two-man bathysphere reaches a depth of 3,031 feet (924 m).

1948
In trials Auguste Piccard takes a bathyscape to 4,995 feet (1,400 m).

1960
In *Trieste*, Jacques Piccard and Don Walsh investigate the Marianas Trench.

1985–1986
Robert Ballard uses the ROV *Jason Junior*, controlled from the submersible *Alvin*, to explore the interior of the *Titanic*.

ROVs are usually equipped with a video camera, lights, and instruments to record the vessel's depth and geographical position. Ballard has transmitted his ROV explorations live, via the World Wide Web, to schools and aquariums around the world; doing so has allowed others to share in his explorations and discoveries in real time.

AUTONOMOUS SUBMERSIBLES

Although ROVs complement the work of manned submersibles at a fraction of the cost, they have the major disadvantage of being attached to a parent vessel. Efforts are underway to develop so-called autonomous underwater vehicles (AUVs), which would collect data as they travel untethered along a preprogrammed route.

As the twenty-first century began, the Deep Sea Submergence Laboratory at WHOI was building a hybrid ROV (HROV), which is designed to work in two modes. Operating as an ROV, it is linked by thin micro-cables to a parent vessel. In free-swimming mode, powered by batteries lasting up to thirty-six hours, the HROV operates in areas where

cables would hamper progress (under the polar ice, for example). It is hoped that further examination of the deep trenches of the Pacific Ocean by HROVs will yield more information about the earth's crust.

Alvin

*A*lvin was the first untethered manned deep-sea submersible. Named after Allyn Vine, the WHOI engineer who designed and built it, *Alvin* can withstand the crushing pressure of water at depths of up to 14,760 feet (4,500 m). *Alvin* has a titanium hull that measures twenty-three feet, four inches (7 m), and is driven by five hydraulic thrusters that propel it at speeds of between one and two knots. In 1974 *Alvin* worked alongside other submersibles as part of Project FAMOUS (French-American Mid-Ocean Undersea Study), whose goal was to confirm theories of seafloor spreading along the Mid-Atlantic Ridge. In 1977 *Alvin* discovered the first hydrothermal vents in the Pacific. To the amazement of scientists, though the water around these vents is sulfurous, with temperatures reaching several hundred degrees Celsius, hydrothermal vents are home to thriving ecosystems. Locating the wreck of the *Titanic* in 1985 was among *Alvin's* most publicized achievements, but as the vessel still makes some 150 to 200 dives every year, perhaps *Alvin's* most exciting discoveries are still to come.

Left This fissure was caused by volcanic activity at a midocean ridge in the Pacific Ocean. At a depth of 8,530 feet (2,600 m), crabs thrive in the warm currents swirling around the fissure.

SEE ALSO

- Cousteau, Jacques-Yves
- Earth
- Underwater Exploration

SURVEYS

A SURVEY IS A DETAILED EXAMINATION of an area of land. Surveys have been conducted with a range of tools and for a number of purposes, including the establishment of boundaries, the location of valuable mineral deposits, and the planning of large-scale construction projects.

Right **This 1930 photograph shows surveyors in northern Iraq using a plane table and an alidade.**

WHY ARE SURVEYS MADE?

There are three main reasons to survey land. The first is the official and legal establishment of the boundary between one landowner's property and another's. To make appropriate use of property, a landowner must know precisely where it begins and ends.

A survey may also determine whether an area of land is worth mining for valuable minerals, such as precious metals, gemstones, or fossil fuels. Modern surveyors use radar technology to locate underground mineral deposits and sonar devices for underwater surveying projects.

A third reason for surveying land is to determine the feasibility of large-scale construction projects. Civil engineers depend on land surveys to ensure the safe (and profitable) construction of dams, transmission lines, canals, bridges, tunnels, and other similar structures. Agricultural engineers laying out irrigation channels to bring water to crops need to know, for reasons of economy, how their farmland slopes. Water flows naturally downhill but requires expensive pumping machinery to carry it uphill.

A land survey is an essential component in the planning and construction of transport infrastructure. Without surveys the construction of the American railroads—which, in the nineteenth century, did much to open up the western United States to widespread settlement—would have been impossible. Before the route of a railroad could be laid out, it was essential for surveyors to establish the gradient (slope) of the land, since a steam-powered locomotive was not able to climb too steep an incline.

SURVEYING TECHNOLOGY

Surveyors' findings are often represented in the form of maps. Not surprisingly, surveyors use many tools that are also used by mapmakers. One of the most important tools for surveyors and mapmakers alike is the magnetic compass. The compass was used in its most primitive form (a piece of magnetized rock) by Chinese surveyors and mapmakers in the third century BCE and had come into use in Europe by the twelfth century CE. Ancient Greek mapmakers and surveyors used an astrolabe to plot out the location of features on the ground with reference to the position of the sun or stars. At the beginning of the seventeenth century, other surveying instruments came into use. They included the plane table (a tripod-mounted drawing board on which measurements are recorded) and the alidade, a telescopic device for calculating the height of distant objects.

Many modern surveyors use photogrammetry, a method of measuring and mapping land features using aerial photography. The extreme accuracy of modern surveying is made possible by instruments that use laser beams as precise measuring tools and by location devices that use data from satellites to establish geographical position.

Gunter's Chain

Named after its inventor, the English mathematician Edmund Gunter (1581–1626), Gunter's chain, also known as the surveyor's chain, is one of the most important surveying tools ever devised. Gunter's chain measured exactly sixty-six feet (21.1 m) in length and was divided into one hundred links. Ten square chains are equal to one acre. In the United States and Canada, the acre remains the basic surveyor's unit of measurement (Gunter's heavy chains were replaced by steel tape in the early 1900s).

Below **Engineers planning major construction projects depend on the work of surveyors. This bridge, pictured during construction in 1895, was built at Arcata, California.**

Right **This Egyptian wall painting, which dates from around 1500 BCE, depicts ancient surveyors using rope to measure farmland.**

SURVEYS IN THE ANCIENT WORLD

The pyramids of ancient Egypt (built between around 2650 and 1550 BCE) provide compelling evidence of the surveying skills of the ancient Egyptians. Despite their vast proportions, the pyramids are contructed with geometrical precision. The Great Pyramid of Khufu is 480 feet (146 m) high and has a practically perfect square base, aligned on an exact north-south line, whose sides measure 755 feet (230 m).

The ancient Egyptians (in common with the ancient Sumerians) also surveyed land for the purpose of establishing property boundaries, particularly of famers' fields. Delineated areas, having been measured with a rope of an agreed length, were marked on the ground with boundary stones.

SURVEYING THE UNITED STATES

The systematic surveying of the United States was an instrumental stage in the for-mation of the nation. The huge undertaking began in 1785 in East Liverpool, Ohio, when Thomas Hutchins (1730–1789) started to map out the country using Edmund Gunter's sixty-six-foot (21.1 m) chain as a basic unit of measurement. As the official geographer to the United States, Hutchins laid out the vast invisible grid of chains and acres that makes up the country's three million square miles. Throughout the nineteenth century, without reference to this grid, no land could be valued, owned, bought, or sold. Most city blocks in the United States are still measured out in accordance with Gunter's chain system.

EXPLORING FOR OIL

Surveyors prospecting (searching) for oil start by examining large areas of land, often by means of an aerial survey. If certain features of the terrain suggest that oil lies beneath the surface, geological surveyors move in for a closer look. Oil is usually found in rocks that were once underwater, so surveyors examine rocks for any evidence of marine life. Indicators include fossils of ancient sea creatures or marks left by sea creatures as they burrowed into the rock.

The next stage after a geological survey is usually a seismic test. Shock waves, either from an explosion or a loud noise, are directed into the ground, and the echoes are picked up by microphones placed at regular intervals leading away from the source of the sound. The pattern and nature of these echoes, when analyzed by experts, may suggest the presence or absence of oil. If the results suggest that oil is present, samples are retrieved from the rocks by drilling.

Surveying Mount Everest

*I*n the early nineteenth century the British launched the Great Trigonometrical Survey of India. In 1790 surveyors who sighted the Himalayas wondered if the distant peaks might be the highest mountains in the world. Closer examination was impossible, since the surrounding areas—Tibet, Nepal, China, Sikkim, and Bhutan—were out of bounds to Europeans. Consequently, measurements had to be carried out from a distance of 150 miles (241 km) or more.

In 1856 the survey's head of computing, Radhanath Sikdhar, announced the discovery of the highest mountain in the world. Although the local Tibetan name for the mountain was Chomolungma ("goddess mother of the world"), the surveyors elected to call it first Peak B, then Peak XV, and finally Mount Everest, after the recently retired superintendent of the survey, Colonel George Everest. The mountain's name remains the same, despite recent attempts to reinstate its Tibetan name.

Left The theodolite, a telescope mounted so that it swivels both horizontally and vertically, gives precise angular measurements. The one pictured here was used by George Everest during the nineteenth-century survey of India.

SEE ALSO

- Astronomy
- Aviation
- Land Transport
- Mapmaking
- Natural Resources
- Photography
- Remote Sensing
- Satellites
- Underground Exploration
- Underwater Exploration

TASMAN, ABEL

THE VOYAGES OF ABEL TASMAN (c. 1603–c. 1659) are among the Netherlands' most significant contributions to the history of exploration. Tasman transformed European knowledge of the lands between the southern Indian and Pacific Oceans from sketches, guesswork, and fantasy into something approaching a clear picture of the dimensions of Australia and New Zealand.

Below **A seventeenth-century portrait of Abel Tasman, one of the greatest Dutch explorers.**

EMERGING DUTCH POWER

Abel Janszoon Tasman was born in Lutjegast, a village in the northern Netherlands, at the dawn of a Dutch golden age. As a young man he was employed as an ordinary sailor in Amsterdam, the bustling center of the Dutch trading empire. In 1632 or 1633 he entered the service of the Dutch East India Company, whose control of the trade in Southeast Asian luxuries had made the Netherlands one of the richest and most powerful nations in the world.

EAST INDIES

Tasman's three-year contract took him to Batavia (present-day Jakarta, Indonesia). He served, first as a mate and later as a captain, on voyages transporting goods around the network of Dutch trading posts throughout Southeast Asia. In 1639 he captained the *Gracht* on an expedition led by Matthijs Quast to locate the mythical islands Rica de Oro (rich in gold) and Rica de Plata (rich in silver), reputed to lie somewhere east of Japan.

1603
Abel Tasman is born in the northern Netherlands.

c. 1632
In the service of the Dutch East India Company, travels to Batavia.

1639
Searches for mythical islands east of Japan.

AUGUST 14, 1642
Leaves Batavia on a voyage to explore the area between the southern Indian and Pacific Oceans.

DECEMBER 13, 1642
Makes first European sighting of New Zealand.

FEBRUARY 6, 1643
Makes first European sighting of the Fijian Islands.

1644
Explores the southern coast of New Guinea and the northwestern coast of Australia.

1659
Dies a prosperous Batavia merchant.

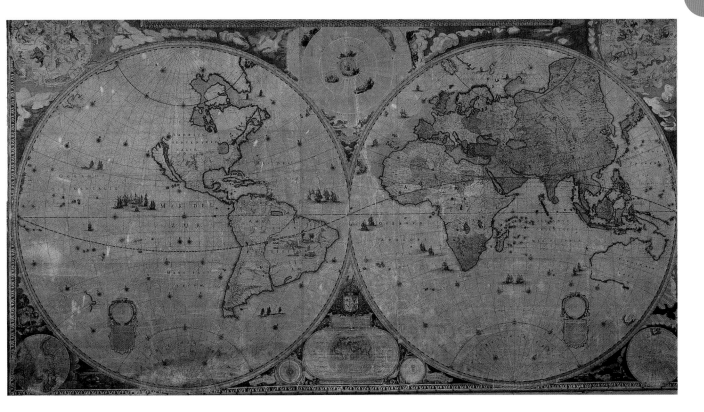

INTO THE UNKNOWN

In 1642 Anthony van Diemen, the governor-general of Dutch East India, appointed Tasman to lead a voyage into the southern Indian Ocean and from there east toward the Pacific. The Dutch knew stretches of the western and southern coast of Australia (a province they called New Holland) but were unsure whether they were part of a single landmass or merely a series of small islands.

On August 14, 1642, Tasman left Batavia with two ships, the *Heemskerck* and the *Zeehean*. He sailed to Mauritius and then into far southern latitudes before bad weather forced him east. On November 24, sailing in uncharted waters south of Australia, he sighted the mountains of a land he named Van Diemen's Land (it was renamed Tasmania in 1853). On December 5, after the ships had skirted the southern coast, a council of officers concluded that Van Diemen's Land was not worth exploring.

On December 13 Tasman became the first European to sight New Zealand. Wondering if he had found the western edge of a vast new continent, he sailed north and, on December 18, anchored his ships at present-day Golden Bay. The following day Maoris (native New Zealanders) approached in canoes. Although the encounter was cordial at first, it descended into a violent skirmish in which four Dutchmen and one Maori were killed.

A Glimpse of Australia

*T*asman's 1642–1643 voyage was piloted by Frans Jacobszoon Visscher, an esteemed hydrographer and surveyor. Visscher's charts offered a tantalizing glimpse of the shape of Australia without entirely dashing hopes of a huge southern continent stretching across the Pacific. Over a century later, between 1768 and 1775, James Cook relied heavily on Visscher's charts when he completed the map of Australia and New Zealand and circumnavigated the world at high southern latitudes—and proved beyond a doubt that no vast southern continent existed.

Above **This world map, drawn in 1655 by the Dutch cartographer Jan Blaeu, represents Tasman's findings. Although much of the Australian outline is complete, the continent's relationship to Tasmania is unknown, and it is wrongly joined to New Guinea. The eastward extent of New Zealand was also unknown. Until the voyages of James Cook, many thought that land filled the entire South Pacific.**

Right **The circular sweep of Tasman's voyage, which touched land at Tasmania, New Zealand, Tonga, and Fiji, added much to Dutch knowledge of southern waters.**

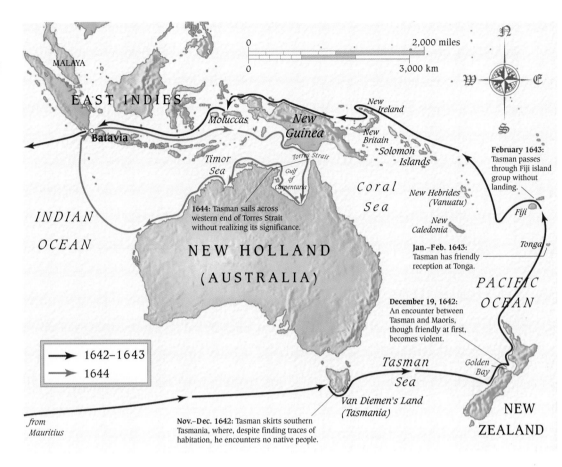

Heading northeast, Tasman reached Tonga on January 21, 1643, and on February 6 was the first European to sight Fiji. From there he turned northwest into familiar New Guinea waters and arrived back in Batavia on June 15.

The Naming of New Zealand

When Tasman sighted New Zealand, he conjectured that he found the western coast of *Terra Australis*, a vast southern continent. A possible eastern edge had been found 4,500 miles (7,240 km) away, at the tip of South America, by two Dutchmen, Willem Schouten and Jakob le Maire, in 1616.

Schouten and Le Maire named their discovery Staten Landt, and in 1642 Tasman gave his discovery the same name, in the hope that the two places were joined. His hope was dashed only a few months later when Hendrik Brouwer, another Dutchman, sailed south of Le Maire's Staten Landt and thus proved that it was only a small island. By the late 1640s the name New Zealand was in use (the Dutch province of Zeeland was second only to the province of Holland in importance).

Despite the discoveries Tasman made, as the exact geography of New Holland remained a mystery, the voyage was considered a failure. In 1644 Van Diemen sent Tasman to investigate the area south and east of New Guinea. Although Tasman failed to identify the Torres Strait (which separates New Guinea from Australia), he charted the Gulf of Carpentaria and a considerable stretch of the northern Australian coast.

LATER LIFE

Tasman's failure to find any evidence of wealth discouraged Van Diemen from any further voyages of exploration to the southeast. After a trading voyage in 1647 and an attack on a Spanish treasure ship in 1648, Tasman spent the remainder of his life working as a merchant in Batavia.

SEE ALSO

• Cook, James • Netherlands • Southern Continent

THOMPSON, DAVID

GENERALLY CELEBRATED AS CANADA'S GREATEST GEOGRAPHER, David Thompson (1770–1857) worked as a fur trader and surveyor. On journeys that covered over 55,000 miles (90,000 km), Thompson made painstaking surveys and drew remarkably detailed maps of central and western Canada and the present-day northwestern United States.

APPRENTICESHIP

Born into a poor Welsh family living in London, at age fourteen David Thompson was selected by the Hudson's Bay Company to become an apprentice clerk. Shortly afterward he sailed to Canada to take up his position. The Hudson's Bay Company traded fur, mainly from beaver but also from other animals, purchased from Native American trappers. In search of new sources of fur, traders traveled deep into unexplored wilderness, far from settled areas. The risks were high but so were the profits.

In May 1784 Thompson began training at Fort Churchill, on the western coast of Hudson Bay. During his first years with the Hudson's Bay Company, he traveled along the North Saskatchewan River as far as Manchester House, a trading post around forty-two miles (68 km) northwest of present-day North Battleford.

For a year Thompson worked alongside the explorer Samuel Hearne. A near-fatal accident in December 1788 changed the course of Thompson's career. While out trapping near Manchester House, he fell and broke his leg. The break was serious, and it took a whole year for Thompson to recover (he limped for the rest of his life).

Thompson spent the following winter downriver at Fort Cumberland and took the opportunity to study under Philip Turnor, the Hudson's Bay Company surveyor. For the first time Thompson handled sextants, telescopes, and other surveying instruments. In February 1790 he took his first positional measurement. At the same time he began learning some local Native American languages.

Below **Thompson spent his first year in Canada at Fort Churchill, near this bend in the Churchill River. He traveled around in a Native American birchbark canoe much like this one.**

THE SURVEYOR

By summer 1790 Thompson was using his new skills to survey the coast of Hudson Bay. Between 1793 and 1796 he traveled extensively in the region of Reindeer Lake and mapped the Saskatchewan, Hayes, Nelson, Churchill, and Reindeer Rivers. In 1795 he was appointed surveyor for the Hudson's Bay Company, and in the spring of 1796, by traveling up the Black River, he found a quicker route to fur-rich Athabasca country than the one previously known. Although for Thompson, surveying was of primary interest, the Hudson's Bay Company placed greater emphasis on trade. Therefore, in the summer of 1797 Thompson transferred to the North West Company, the Hudson's Bay Company's great rival.

THE NORTH WEST YEARS

Thompson's first assignment for the North West Company was to map the area between the Red, Missouri, and Mississippi Rivers. In his first year with the company, Thompson traveled over four thousand miles (6,500 km). First he journeyed from the Missouri to the Mississippi, and then he surveyed the south-

Left **The English explorer Samuel Hearne (1745–1792) was the first European to travel overland to the Arctic Ocean.**

APRIL 30, 1770
David Thompson is born in London.

1784
Sails for Canada as an apprentice of the Hudson's Bay Company.

1788
Breaks his leg near Manchester House.

1789–1790
Studies to become a surveyor for the Hudson's Bay Company.

1795
Becomes chief surveyor for the Hudson's Bay Company.

1796
Finds a quick route to Athabasca country.

1797
Joins the North West Company.

1799
Marries Charlotte Small.

1801
While stationed at Rocky Mountain House, seeks a safe passage through the Rocky Mountains.

1806
Discovers the Howse Pass in the Rocky Mountains.

1812
Retires from the North West Company and settles near Montreal.

1814
Completes maps of Canada's Northwest Territories.

1816
Working alongside the International Boundary Commission, helps to establish the border separating Canada from the United States.

1847
Begins writing *David Thompson's Narrative*.

FEBRUARY 10, 1857
Dies in Montreal.

The Sextant

In 1791 Thompson purchased a brass sextant, an instrument for measuring the position of a given celestial body relative to the horizon. Invented in 1757, the sextant consists of an arc that subtends an angle of one-sixth of a circle. Capable of measuring angles up to 120 degrees, the sextant has a telescope and two mirrors; one is half-silvered, and the other is fully reflective.

To take a reading, the navigator looks at the horizon through the telescope and the half-silvered mirror. The other mirror, mounted on a moveable arm, is angled until a given star is reflected onto the mirrored portion of the half-mirror. The navigator makes minute adjustments until, viewed through the telescope, the reflected star appears exactly level with the horizon. The angle between the horizon and the star can then be read off the scale. With this information, the navigator can consult a lunar table to establish the exact latitude of his position.

Left **This brass sextant was made by George Adams (1750–1795), a London instrument maker.**

ern shoreline of Lake Superior to Sault Sainte Marie before traveling east to Grand Portage (in present-day Minnesota).

PASSAGE THROUGH THE ROCKIES

In 1799 Thompson married Charlotte Small, the thirteen-year-old half-Cree daughter of a fellow fur trapper. Thompson took Charlotte with him on most of his subsequent trips. In 1806 he discovered the Howse Pass through the Rocky Mountains near the source of the Columbia River. With this discovery Thompson opened up a trade route from Canada to the Pacific.

By 1810 Thompson had surveyed many parts of present-day Montana, Idaho, Oregon, Washington, and British Columbia. In 1811 he began exploring the Columbia River system and surveyed much of what is now the U.S.-Canadian border.

A GREAT MAP

Thompson retired from the North West Company in 1812 and settled at Terrebonne, north of Montreal. He compiled the information he had gathered on his travels and created a map of the Northwest Territories of Canada. Completed in 1814, Thompson's map was so accurate that it was still in use over a hundred years later.

In 1815 Thompson moved from Terrebone to Williamstown, Ontario. From 1818 to 1836 he headed the International Boundary Commission, which surveyed the border between Canada and the United States. By 1833, however, after a series of business failures and the collapse of the North West Company—in which he still held shares—Thompson was left bankrupt. In 1847, in spite of his failing eyesight, he began writing about his travels in a book with the simple title *David Thompson's Narrative*. Thompson died in poverty in 1857 before he could finish his work.

Below **An 1871 depiction of a Hudson's Bay Company trading station in Manitoba, Canada.**

Thompson's acccount of his travels revealed a sensitive man who discovered as much about the life and customs of Native Americans as he did about the geography of their homeland:

After a weary day's march we sat by a log fire, the bright Moon, with thousands of sparkling stars passing before us, we could not help enquiring who lived in those bright mansions; for I frequently conversed with them [native Americans] as one of themselves; the brilliancy of the planets always attracted their attention, and when their nature was explained to them, they concluded them to be the abodes of the spirits of those that had led a good life . . .

David Thompson, *Narrative of His Explorations in Western America 1784–1812*

SEE ALSO

- La Vérendrye, Pierre Gaultier de Varennes de
- Lewis and Clark Expedition
- Mackenzie, Alexander

TIDES AND CURRENTS

A NAVIGATOR'S UNDERSTANDING OF TIDES AND CURRENTS was often the determining factor in the success or failure of a maritime voyage. Just as a miscalculation or an incomplete understanding of tides and currents led in many instances to tragedy, so the ability to use tides and currents to advantage or even the chance discovery of a previously unknown tide or current led in many cases to a discovery of major importance.

Left **By mastering the formidable power of the ocean, sailors and navigators were able to travel far from home and thus to initiate the discovery and exploration of distant lands.**

WHAT IS A TIDE?

The gravitational attraction of the moon (and, to a lesser extent, the sun) causes the waters on those parts of the earth facing directly toward and directly away from the moon to bulge. The daily rotation of the earth through these bulges creates high and low tides, the ebb and flow of water observed along the coastlines of the world.

Although the difference between high and low tide varies around the world, it averages between six and ten feet (2–3 m). The world's widest range between high and low tide, forty feet (12 m), occurs at the Bay of Fundy in Canada. Tidal action in the Mediterranean, Baltic, and Caribbean Seas is very much lower.

WHAT IS A CURRENT?

A current is a continuous flow of water in a particular direction. Surface currents are caused by the drag exerted upon a body of water by prevailing winds. Ocean currents have been described as "rivers within the seas." Some travel several thousand miles and influence the climate and ecology of the areas they travel through. The Gulf Stream, for example, carries warm waters from the Gulf of Mexico to Newfoundland and across the North Atlantic to the British Isles and Norway. This warm current helps to keep the waters of northern Europe from freezing in winter. Palm trees and other tropical plants grow in sheltered bays in Cornwall and western Scotland.

Importance of Tides and Currents

Before the invention of steam-powered ships in the nineteenth century, it was essential that a seafarer have detailed knowledge of ocean currents. If a sailing ship became caught in a slow-moving current or tried to sail against a current, the journey time would lengthen, and the crew would be at risk of running out of food or fresh drinking water.

Even after sails were superseded by steam engines, tides and currents continued to play a vital role in international shipping. International maritime trade is conducted via a network of harbors and ports, places where ships dock and unload or take on cargo. The construction of such ports involves dredging deep harbor basins and building huge moles (harbor walls) that limit the effect of tides on ships as they perform complicated maneuvers in and out of dock.

Early Explanations of Tides

Some ancient Indian writers believed that the tides were caused by the rhythmic breathing of an immense underwater sea god. During the second century BCE the Greek astronomer Seleucus of Babylon was probably the first thinker to make a connection between the tides and the moon. He believed that the pressure exterted by the moon on the earth's atmosphere caused the wind and oceans to move. Chinese and Arabic scholars also recorded the connection between the rise and fall of the tides and the monthly passage of the moon.

The monks who lived in the monastery on Holy Island (also known as Lindisfarne) from around 635 to 875 CE had practical reasons for observing and measuring the ebb and flow of the sea. The island, off the coast of Northumberland in north-

Right **Constructed in 1580, this tide predictor enables the user to determine the time of high tide at a particular port from the age of the moon, provided the location of the port is known. The device is also used for telling the time at night.**

The Tidal Dock at Lothal

*T*he need for harbors that are deep enough for ships to berth at low tide without running aground was appreciated as much in ancient times as in modern. Archaeologists investigating the Harappan civilization, which flourished in the Indus valley in northern India, have found evidence that, around the year 2500 BCE, a tidal dock was constructed at Lothal, at the head of the Gulf of Cambay. Measuring 121 feet (37 m) long and 72 feet (22 m) wide, the dockyard held up to sixty ships. Ships entered the dock from the nearby Sabarmati River at high tide. The dock gates were then closed to retain the water until the ships were unloaded. Channels carried away excess water and river silt. Evidence found in the surrounding wharf and its warehouses suggests that Harappan ships explored and traded widely in the seas around Arabia and India.

eastern England, is cut off from the mainland at high tide and can be reached only at low tide by a causeway. Perhaps unsurprisingly, one of the most detailed early medieval scientific studies of the sea was penned by the Northumbrian scholar the Venerable Bede (673–735).

MEASURING TIDES

The Tsien Tang River, in eastern China, has long been famous for its tidal bore, a thirty-foot (9 m) wall of water that rushes up the river at high tide and, in the past, has caused serious problems for river traffic. As early as the eleventh century, Chinese scholars drew up a table to record and predict the tidal bore. According to ancient local legend, the thunderous tidal waves were caused by the angry spirit of Wu Tsu-Hsu, a murdered general. (In fact, tidal bores result from a compression effect that occurs when, at a narrow area of a low-lying river near the river's mouth, a fast-rising incoming tide meets water flowing out of the river.)

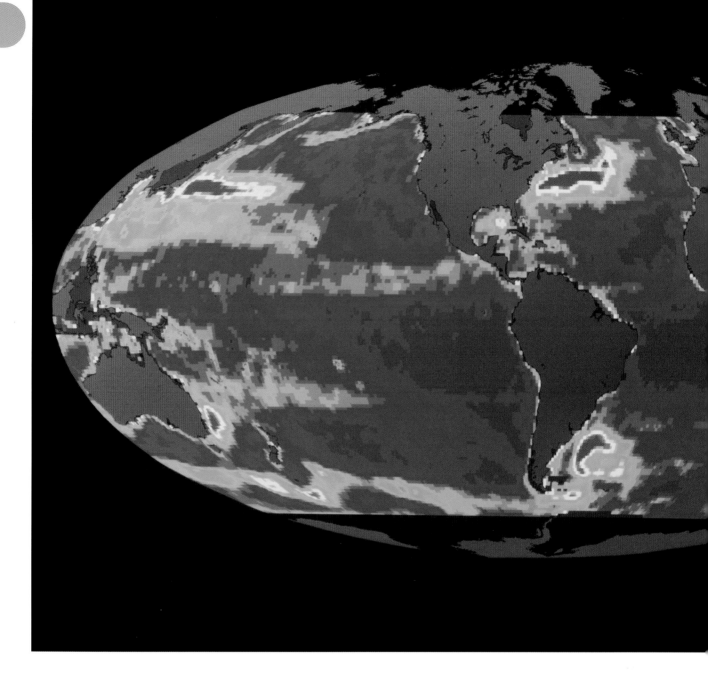

Above **This map was drawn from data collected by the *Geosat* satellite from 1987 to 1988. The world's major ocean currents, shown in red, are (clockwise from top left) the Kiro Shio current, the Gulf Stream, the Agulhas current, the Brazil current, and the East Australian current.**

The first written tide table for European waters recorded the "flod at london brigge" (high water at London Bridge) in the thirteenth century. By the sixteenth century English and French sea captains could purchase almanacs that listed the so-called flood moons (times of high tide) at various important harbors and ports. Sailors working at the port of King's Lynn in Norfolk (in eastern England) were also helped by the tide clock on the spire of Saint Margaret's Church. Built in 1681, the clock displayed the local high tide throughout the lunar month of twenty-nine and a half days.

Though numerous scholars were able to measure and predict high and low tides, a true understanding of the underlying cause of tides did not emerge until the eighteenth century, when the theory of gravity proposed by the English scientist Isaac Newton (1642–1727) began to gain widespread acceptance. The Swiss mathematicians Daniel Bernoulli (1700–1782) and Leonhard Euler (1707–1783) and the French scientist Pierre-Simon de Laplace (1749–1827) produced the first explanations of tides with reference to the effect of the moon's gravitational pull on the earth's oceans and seas.

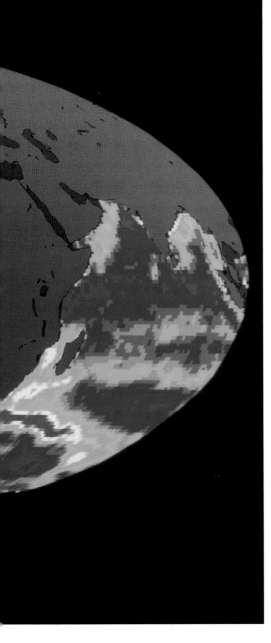

CURRENTS AND CONQUEST

Currents both helped and hindered the exploration of the world's oceans. Ancient Polynesian navigators knew that the currents in the Pacific Ocean north of the equator flowed in a different direction from those to its south. They used their knowledge to undertake vast journeys, sometimes thousands of miles long, in simple canoes. Around 1000 CE the Viking explorer Leif Eriksson used the westward summer currents of the North Atlantic to sail from Iceland to Greenland.

In the fifteenth century Portuguese sailors had great difficulty sailing down the Atlantic coast of Africa; strong prevailing southerly winds and matching currents pushed their ships north as they tried to sail south. Bartolomeu Dias pioneered a slanting course that detoured west into midocean before turning back east toward the southern tip of Africa. (While taking this route in 1500, the Portuguese explorer Pedro Álvares Cabral was blown off course and became the first European to land in Brazil).

By the early sixteenth century Spanish captains had found a quick route from their New World colonies in the Americas back to Spain via the Gulf Stream, or North Atlantic Drift, a fast current that, in places, flows at over three miles per hour (4.8 kph) and runs from the Gulf of Mexico to northern Europe. In 1542 the Spanish navigator Bernard de le Torre discovered the westward-flowing North Equatorial Current in the Pacific Ocean. These currents and others were instrumental in helping the Spanish and later imperial European powers to run global empires.

SEE ALSO

- Cabral, Pedro Álvares • Ships and Boats
- Underwater Exploration

TINNÉ, ALEXANDRINE-PIETERNELLA-FRANÇOISE

THE AFRICAN JOURNEYS of Alexandrine-Pieternella-Françoise Tinné (1835–1869) testify to a remarkable courage and a passion to uncover geographical and scientific knowledge about a region of the world that few Europeans had ever explored. Her death at the age of only thirty-four robbed the world of someone who would have continued to break new ground in the fields of exploration and botany.

Below **This portrait of Alexandrine Tinné was drawn by Wilhelm Gentz.**

Alexandrine-Pieternella-Françoise Tinné was born in the Hague in the Netherlands on October 17, 1835. Her parents, Philip F. Tinn and Baroness Henrietta van Steengracht-Capellan, devoted some of their considerable wealth to sponsoring botanists, and Alexandrine developed an interest in botany from an early age.

TRAVELING WITH A PURPOSE

In 1861, at age twenty-six, Tinné left Europe and traveled to Cairo. She began to plan an expedition deep into the heart of East Africa, a region visited by very few Europeans—let alone European women.

Tinné's aims were to record the geography and flora and fauna of the upper Nile basin and perhaps to locate the source of the Nile. In addition, Tinné shared the hope of many nineteenth-century explorers of Africa that, by bringing European and American influence to the peoples of the interior, they would hasten the end of the slave trade.

1835
Alexandrine-Pieternella-Françoise Tinné is born in the Hague.

1861
Arrives in Cairo.

1862
Travels to Khartoum; explores the Sobat River.

1863–1864
Explorers the headwaters of the Nile.

1867
Plantes Tinnéennes is published.

1869
Tinné is murdered.

IN THE HEART OF AFRICA

Tinné was joined in Cairo by her mother, her aunt, several scientists, more than two hundred servants, and some one hundred camels. The expedition left the Egyptian capital on January 9, 1862, and traveled south to Khartoum, the present-day capital of Sudan, which is situated at the confluence of the Blue Nile and the White Nile.

Theodor von Heuglin *1824–1876*

A scientist-explorer in the tradition of his great compatriot Alexander von Humboldt (1769–1859), Theodor von Heuglin traveled throughout northeastern Africa in the 1850s and, from 1857, served as Austrian consul at Khartoum. In 1863 Heuglin joined Alexandrine Tinné's exploration party. He returned to Europe in 1864 and in 1865 published an account of his journey with Tinné. His books about the wildlife of northeastern Africa gained him considerable renown as an ornithologist and zoologist. In 1870 and 1871 he led expeditions to Spitsbergen and Novaya Zemlya, Arctic island groups. In 1875 he returned to northeastern Africa. He died the following year while preparing for an exploration of Socotra, an island in the Arabian Sea east of the Horn of Africa.

From Khartoum the party continued up the White Nile by steamship to Gondokoro, the farthest point of navigation. Tinné had planned to meet the British explorer John Hanning Speke, but when he did not arrive, she continued with her exploration. She traveled northeast and explored the Sobat River, a major tributary of the White Nile. Traveling for long stretches on horseback, according to contemporary reports, she was dressed so ornately that she was mistaken by local people for a sultan's daughter.

In November, Tinné returned to Khartoum, where there was still no sign of Speke. In February 1863 she was joined by two German explorers, Theodor von Heuglin and Hermann Steudner. The party traveled south and west along the Bahr al-Ghazal (Gazelle River), another major tributary of the White Nile, in an attempt to establish the westward extent of the Nile basin and investigate reports of a vast lake in central Africa to the east of those already known (the reports probably referred to lakelike stretches of the Congo River).

Above **At the head of an expedition party numbering several hundred, Tinné cut an imperious figure, as this 1869 engraving suggests.**

SCIENTIFIC FINDINGS

Tinné returned to Cairo, where she lived for four years. The publication of the findings of her expedition brought her much acclaim. A description of some of the plants she had gathered, published in Vienna in 1867 as *Plantes Tinnéennes,* included twenty-four new species and a whole new genus, named *Tinnea,* of tropical mint.

FATAL EXPEDITION

Tinné settled in Algiers in 1867. In January 1869 she set out from Tripoli (the Libyan capital) in a caravan heading for Lake Chad. Had she completed the journey, she would have been the first European woman to cross the Sahara Desert. However, on August 1 she made a detour to visit a Tuareg encampment and en route was murdered by Tuaregs. The reason for her tragic death remains a mystery. It is possible that her attackers believed that her iron water tanks were filled with gold.

Continuing southwest, the party explored the region that divides the drainage basins of the Nile and Congo Rivers. All members succumbed to fever, and many lost their life. In April, Steudner died, and in June, Tinné's mother died. In July 1864 the remainder of the expedition arrived back in Khartoum, where Tinné's aunt also died.

SEE ALSO

TRADE

OF ALL THE REASONS for which humans have ventured out on journeys of exploration, none has been more important than trade. From the time of the earliest civilizations, people were compelled or inspired to seek out new territory by the promise of new commodities, whether luxuries or staples. Many of the great feats of exploration were undertaken by traders or in the name of trade, and from the sixteenth century on, merchant companies played a leading role in sponsoring voyages of exploration.

Left **This Egyptian tomb painting of around 1500 BCE depicts workers loading a ship with wheat, which was traded for cedar wood, silver, and iron in western Asia and for ivory, copper, animal skins, and spices in Nubia, Egypt's neighbor to the south.**

EARLY TRADERS

Archaeological evidence indicates that, as long as five thousand years ago, the ancient civilizations of Egypt, Mesopotamia (present-day Iraq), and the Indus valley were trading with each other over long distance, by land as well as by sea. (Nothing is known, however, of the explorers who pioneered the trade routes that were used.) Perhaps the greatest seafaring traders of the ancient world were the Phoenicians. Despite a relatively small homeland (which corresponds roughly to present-day Lebanon), the Phoenicians' control of Mediterranean trade won them great power and influence in the first millennium BCE. It is possible that Phoenician seafarers sailed around Africa in the sixth century BCE, and they almost certainly traveled as far as the Azores (a mid-Atlantic island group) and southwestern Britain, where they traded for tin (used in the manufacture of bronze).

Between the ninth and eleventh centuries CE, Vikings sailed south from Scandinavia along the rivers of Russia and penetrated as far as Constantinople (present-day Istanbul, in Turkey), where they traded with the Byzantine Empire. Vikings also sailed west across the North Sea and the North Atlantic, in search of new farmland and other natural resources, and reached Iceland, Greenland, and North America.

Right **In the early fifteenth century a French artist painted this imaginary picture of the Bay of Cambay, on the northwestern coast of India. The wealth of Cambay had been described in the fourteenth century by Marco Polo, who wrote, "Many merchant ships call here with various imports, especially gold, silver and brass."**

TRADE BETWEEN EUROPE AND ASIA

By the first century BCE luxury goods, such as silk and jade, were being carried west from China overland along a number of trade routes known collectively as the Silk Road. During the thirteenth century CE Marco Polo, a Venetian trader, traveled east along the Silk Road from Europe and spent many years in China.

During the Age of Discovery (from around 1490 to 1540), Marco Polo's descriptions of the wealth of China inspired European powers to sponsor numerous significant voyages to search for a direct sea route to East Asia. Indeed, the desire to control the trade in Asian luxuries—by finding a direct route to their source—was the single most important motivating factor in the history of European exploration.

SPICES

During the Middle Ages, the spices of Southeast Asia and India, particularly nutmeg, cloves, mace, cinnamon and pepper, were among the most valuable trade goods in Europe. Spices were transported to gateway cities, such as Cairo and Constantinople, where they were bought by traders, especially Italians from Genoa and Venice. By the time the spices reached European markets, their

route to India was within reach. The culmination of their program of exploration was Vasco da Gama's 1497–1498 voyage to India.

Portuguese successes encouraged the Spanish to sponsor voyages of their own. Christopher Columbus's insistence that Asia could be reached by sailing west across the Atlantic eventually won support. The unexpected result was the discovery, in 1492, of the Americas. The western route to Asia was eventually pioneered by Ferdinand Magellan on a voyage that lasted from 1519 to 1522. The first circumnavigation of the world revealed the vast extent of the Pacific and the difficulty of reaching Asia by a Pacific route.

From the sixteenth century northern European powers began to search for northern routes to Asia. In the process of searching for a northeast passage over the top of Russia and a northwest passage over or through North America, British, Russian, French, Scandinavian, and Dutch explorers discovered valuable new sources of wealth, including cod in the waters off Newfoundland, whales in the Arctic, and furs in the North American and Russian wildernesses.

price increased by as much as a hundredfold, and the Genoese and Venetians were greatly enriching themselves. European powers, led by the Spanish and the Portuguese, reasoned that, by reaching the source of the spices and bringing them to Europe themselves, they would see a similar order of profit.

NEW ROUTES

In the fifteenth century Portuguese ships sailed down the Atlantic coast of Africa, where they traded for gold, ivory, pepper, and slaves. In 1488, after Bartolomeu Dias rounded the southern tip of Africa, the Portuguese realized that their goal of opening a direct sea

Trading Rivalry

From the sixteenth century until the nineteenth, many European governments embraced an economic philosophy that later became known as mercantilism. Mercantilism was based on the belief that the wealth of a nation was measured in the amount of bullion (gold and silver) it owned. In order to maximize its wealth, a nation needed a monopoly, an exclusive right to buy and sell a particular commodity in a given area.

In practice, mercantilist policies resulted in the conquest and colonization of overseas territories and the use of considerable force to prevent the peoples of those territories from trading with any nation other than the colonizer. By the eighteenth century England, Spain, Portugal, the Netherlands, and France all had overseas empires and were all engaged more or less permanently in wars among themselves.

The Dutch East India Company

To avoid having to compete with each other, in 1602 several Dutch companies trading in Asia joined to form the Vereenigde Oost-Indische Compagnie (United East India Company), or VOC. The VOC sent great fleets to the East to seize control of the spice trade.

By 1619 the VOC had conquered the islands that produced most of the world's supply of cloves, mace, and nutmeg. The Dutch then drove the Portuguese and English out of Indonesia, Malaya and Sri Lanka. The VOC has been called the world's first multinational company. In its refusal to accept that the Dutch government had any authority over it, the VOC was essentially a

Below **The exploration of North America was driven to a great extent by hunters of beaver, such as the one depicted in this 1858 painting. The artist, Alfred Jacob Miller, was also an explorer and had seen such scenes at first hand during an 1837 expedition through the Rocky Mountains.**

Left In 1497 the Italian explorer John Cabot, attempting to find a new trade route to China, accidentally discovered the rich cod fishing grounds off Newfoundland. This early-nineteenth-century French painting shows the cod being dried before being shipped to Europe.

state within a state. It had its own army and navy and reserved the right to make treaties, wage wars, and establish colonies.

THE TRADE IN BEAVER FUR

The most prized tradable North American commodity was the fur of the beaver, which was made into felt for hats that were fashionable across Europe in the 1600s and 1700s. Much of the initial exploration of Canada was carried out by fur-trading companies, especially the English-owned Hudson's Bay Company, founded in 1670, and its great rival, the North West Company, set up in 1783. Many of Canada's most successful explorers, including Henry Kelsey and Alexander Mackenzie, were members of these companies. Owing to the lucrative fur trade, by the

This message was delivered by the directors of the Dutch East India Company to the Dutch government in 1644:

The places and strongholds which they have captured in the East Indies should not be regarded as national conquests but as the property of private merchants, who were entitled to sell those places to whomsoever they wished, even it was to the King of Spain or to some other enemy.

Quoted in C. R. Boxer,
The Dutch Seaborne Empire, 1600–1800

1830s the North American beaver had almost disappeared. It was saved from extinction only by a new fashion for silk hats.

SEE ALSO

- Columbus, Christopher
- Gama, Vasco da
- Mackenzie, Alexander
- Magellan, Ferdinand
- Mercantilism
- Natural Resources
- Northeast Passage
- Northwest Passage
- Polo, Marco
- Portugal
- Silk Road
- Spain

618–907 CE
Traders regularly travel along the Silk Road.

c. 870
Viking traders reach the Black Sea.

1271–1275
Marco Polo travels to China.

1498
Vasco da Gama sails to India.

1520–1521
Ferdinand Magellan crosses the Pacific.

1557
The Portuguese set up a trading colony at Macao, off China.

1602
The Dutch East India Company (VOC) is founded.

1611
Spitsbergen becomes a base for European whalers.

1640
The Dutch capture Malacca from the Portuguese.

1670
The Hudson's Bay Company is formed.

1783
The North West Company is founded.

Underground Exploration

IN COMMON WITH MANY OTHER FORMS OF EXPLORATION, underground exploration was prompted first by practical need, later by the desire for enrichment, and more recently by the quest for greater knowledge. The first underground explorers unearthed flints for making tools, their successors mined precious metals, and modern archaeologists and cavers venture into the subterranean world to learn more about the history and structure of the planet Earth.

Mining

The earliest underground explorers were the prehistoric excavators who dug up flints to make a variety of tools 100,000 years ago and more. The earliest record of the mining of precious metals dates from around 6,000 years ago, when gold was mined in Egypt and Mesopotamia (present-day Iraq). It is known that there were significant silver mines in eastern Anatolia (part of modern-day Turkey) around 4,000 years ago.

When traders from Phoenicia (present-day Lebanon) reached Spain around 1000 BCE, they found so much silver that their ships could not carry it all home. In the first half of the sixteenth century, during their conquests of the Incas (of Peru) and the Aztecs (of Mexico), the Spanish themselves discovered large reserves of silver and gold in the Americas. Rumors spread of a fabulously rich kingdom ruled by a king, El Dorado (Spanish for "the gilded one"), who was so wealthy that he painted himself gold. Conquistadores flocked to the New World to find their fortune and in the process explored vast tracts of the newly discovered territory.

Revelations from the Underworld

By the seventeenth century scholars were attempting a comprehensive classification of the known world. In 1654 Jacques Gaffarel published *Le monde sousterrein* (The under-

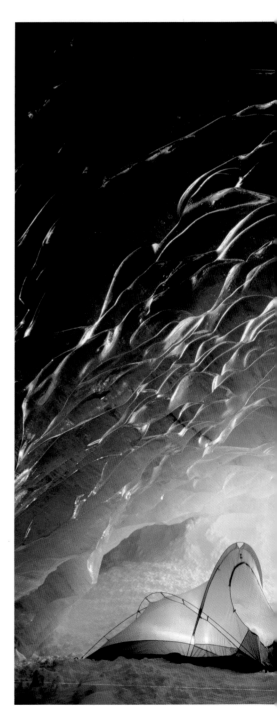

The Roman statesman and philosopher Seneca (4 BCE–65 CE) wrote this memorable description of early mining:

Before the reign of Philip of Macedonia, there were men who set out in search of silver. Unflinchingly, they forced their way into caves, where it is impossible to tell day from night, and resolutely penetrated to the deepest hiding places. To light their way, they took with them large quantities of rushes. The way was long and tiring. They saw huge rushing rivers, and vast still lakes, spectacles fit to make them shake with horror. These men dared to descend into a region where the whole of nature is reversed. The land hung above their heads and the wind whistled hollowly in the shadows. In the depth, the frightful rivers led nowhere into the perpetual and alien night. After accomplishing so much they now live in fear, for having tempted the fires of Hell.

Seneca, *Questions of Nature*

ground world), a description of caves, grottoes, and mines. In 1748 the Holy Roman emperor Francis I sent out his mathematician and physicist J. A. Nagel to examine the Adriatic Sea's limestone coast, which was riddled with caves. Descending four hundred feet (122 m) down into the Mazocha Chasm, Nagel's exploration almost certainly took him deeper than anyone had ever explored before.

In 1860 Édouard-Armand-Isidore-Hippolyte Lartet, a French magistrate, created great excitement when he announced that he had discovered prehistoric remains in a number of caves in southwestern France. Working with an Englishman, Henry Christy, Lartet later uncovered artifacts dating from twelve to fourteen thousand years ago that depicted long-extinct animals. Lartet is credited with being the founder of the science of paleontology, the study of geological remains, particularly fossils of plants and animals, in order to reconstruct the history of the earth.

Left **An explorer photographed beside his tent in an ice cave at the Appa Glacier in British Columbia, in western Canada. In winter a cold wind blows through the cave and freezes the water formed in the summer by melting snow and ice. In summer a cold breeze that blows from the cave depths to the entrance prevents melting.**

Below **This image of a leaping cow and a frieze of small horses, found in the caves at Lascaux, in France, was painted on the rock some 20,000 years ago. It is believed that prehistoric cave art served some form of ritualistic purpose.**

In the wake of Lartet's discovery, archaeologists flocked to caves in search of evidence of early humans. In the summer of 1879, Marcellino de Sautuola visited a cave at Altamira, in northern Spain, with his seven-year-old daughter, Maria. They discovered striking paintings of bison in red, black, and violet colors. However, at the time of Sautuola's death, in 1888, the paintings were generally dismissed as forgeries. It was not until the start of the twentieth century that cave paintings found in France persuaded scientists that prehistoric man was capable of producing such beautiful art as that found in Altamira. Indeed, the Altamira drawings may date from as early as 20,000 BCE and as such are the earliest known examples of Stone Age cave painting.

In 1940 two boys accidentally discovered the cave paintings at Lascaux. Perhaps as much as 17,000 years old, Lascaux is one of the world's most spectacular displays of prehistoric art. The cave was opened as a tourist attraction, but by the early 1960s the paintings were starting to fade as a result of the bright artificial lighting and the humidity from the breath of countless visitors. Noticing that molds and fungi were starting to grow on the cave walls, in 1963 the French Ministry of Culture ordered the cave closed.

1654
Jacques Gaffarel publishes *Le monde sousterrein*.

1748
J. A. Nagel reaches a depth of four hundred feet (122 m) while exploring the karst of the Adriatic coast.

1863
Édouard Lartet and Henry Christy discover prehistoric artifacts in French caves.

1879
Marcellino de Sautuola and his daughter discover cave paintings at Altamira.

1888–1914
Édouard-Alfred Martel explores over a thousand caves and cave passages in Europe.

Karst

*M*ost caves are found in karst, a type of irregular limestone rock eroded by water that has been slightly acidified as it passes through the soil, the acidity producing fissures, sinkholes, underground streams, and caverns. The karst areas of the world are very important as natural reservoirs of water. By 2015, 80 percent of the world's drinkable water is likely to come from karst, so it is extremely desirable that these areas remain protected from pollution.

Above **Speleologists continue to explore one of the world's largest cave systems located in Gunung Mulu National Park, in Sarawak, Malaysia.**

1940
Prehistoric cave paintings are found at Lascaux, in central France.

SPELEOLOGY

The exploration, mapping, and study of the geology and biology of caves is called speleology. The French judge Édouard-Alfred Martel (1859–1938) is credited with making the first speleological expeditions between 1888 and 1914. As a pioneer he had to invent his own equipment, which included a smoking wax candle tucked into his hatband, a series of ladders tied together, and a wooden beam attached to a rope, on which he would sit and be lowered into the depths with a modified winch. With this basic equipment he explored over a thousand caves and underground rivers throughout Europe.

Cavers (or spelunkers, as they are sometimes known) use increasingly sophisticated and lightweight equipment and often live for many weeks in underground camps. Dressed in oversuits, helmets and climbing boots, they light their way using headlamps powered by batteries or calcium carbide—which, when mixed with water, produces a gas that can be burned to give off a bright light. Much of the equipment used by cavers to move up and down rocks is the same as that used by mountaineers. Cavers also use inflatable boats on large underground rivers and wet suits and a variety of diving techniques to explore flooded passages.

SEE ALSO
• Earth

UNDERWATER EXPLORATION

THE OCEANS COVER MORE THAN 70 PERCENT of the earth's surface. For centuries mariners speculated about what lies beneath the surface, but until the twentieth century oceanography (the study of the oceans) could be conducted only from on board a ship. In spite of technological improvements that have enabled explorers to reveal some of the mysteries of the underwater world, the deep sea remains relatively unexplored. Exploration of the deep sea is as technologically challenging and almost as costly as the exploration of space.

Below **The Charles Deane diving suit, patented in 1823, had a hard hat into which oxygen was pumped from a boat on the surface. It was used in shallow water to examine the wreck of the *Mary Rose*.**

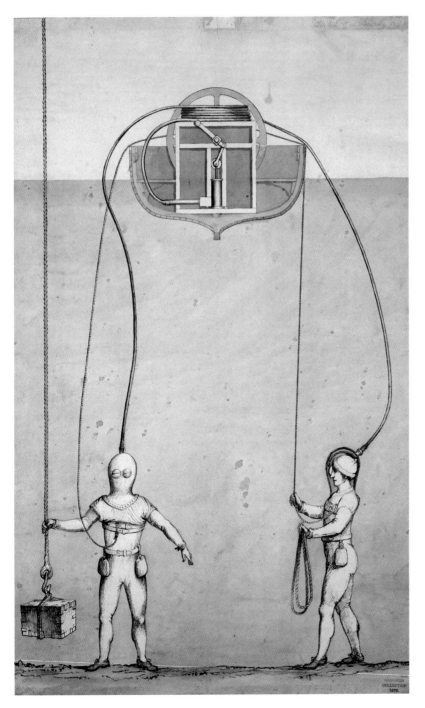

THE NATURE OF THE OCEANS

The continental landmasses are surrounded by a continental shelf, an area of the earth's crust that is covered by shallow seas up to a depth of around 650 feet (200 m). The width of the continental shelf varies greatly around the world but averages around forty miles (65 km). Beyond, a steep continental slope plunges down into an underwater abyss.

EARLY OCEANOGRAPHERS

Until the seventeenth century investigation of the sea was limited to what was of practical use. Mariners exchanged information about the characteristics of coastal waters—specifically, the location of safe anchorages—and on the tides and currents they encountered as they traveled farther from the coast.

In 1660 the Royal Society of London for the Promotion of Natural Knowledge (generally known as the Royal Society) was founded. In 1661 one of its founders, the scientist Robert Boyle (1627–1691), began requesting British seafarers to collect information about the oceans. In France, Luigi Ferdinando Marsili (1658–1730), a geologist, drew up a profile of an area of the seafloor extending from the Mediterranean continental shelf off the French coast out into deeper water. Marsili used the ancient method of taking depth measurements from a boat using a line and

Above **The laying of the transatlantic telegraph cable from the steamship *Great Eastern* in 1865.**

weight, that is, a line with instruments attached to it. Marsili's method remained the principal means of oceanographic investigation for over three hundred years.

Several maritime explorers took measurements of the temperature and salinity of seawater and of patterns of tides and currents. On James Cook's second Pacific voyage (1772–1775), during a circumnavigation of Antarctica scientists discovered that beneath the cold surface of the sea were layers of warmer water. This discovery initiated research into the circulation of water within the oceans. Marine science played an important role in the exploration of the North American Arctic in the nineteenth century.

Cabling beneath the Sea

*I*n 1853 the first international marine conference was held in Brussels, the Belgian capital. Plans to lay an undersea telegraph cable linking Britain with the United States prompted renewed efforts to establish the depth profile of the Atlantic Ocean. Engineers used soundings collected in the 1840s by Matthew Fontaine Maury (1806–1873), an American naval officer, to find the safest routes for the cables. Soon routes were being surveyed for new telegraph cables across the Mediterranean and the Red Sea.

The British mathematician and physicist William Thomson (1824–1907), using steel piano wire, invented a sounding machine that dramatically speeded up mapping of the seabed. Thomson's investigations proved that the sea did not have a flat, muddy bottom but large peaks and troughs, as well as strong currents and marked differences in temperature. Furthermore, living organisms were found attached to cables retrieved from depths of up to 9,840 feet (3,000 m), where it had previously been thought life could not exist.

The British Admiralty hoped that techniques for differentiating between freshwater and salt water would assist them in their attempts to find the Northwest Passage.

Nineteenth-Century Oceanography

During the nineteenth century naturalists investigated the life forms that inhabit the deep ocean by using powerful ships to drag heavy dredges over the ocean floor and then bringing their catch to the surface for examination. Between 1868 and 1870 HMS *Lightning* and *Porcupine* retrieved creatures from depths of up to 3,900 feet (1,190 m). Between 1857 and 1859 the Austro-Hungarian frigate *Novara* circumnavigated the world on a scientific voyage that produced twenty-four volumes of oceanographic information.

In December 1872 HMS *Challenger* set sail from Sheerness, in southeastern England, with five scientific staff under the leadership of Professor Charles Wyville Thomson. By the time the ship returned in May 1876, it had sailed 68,890 miles (110,870 km). Having made 492 soundings and 284 dredges and trawls, the scientists had collected data from all the world's oceans except the Arctic. The information they gathered was published in fifty volumes between 1880 and 1895, and their collection of plants, animals, and deep-sea deposits was housed in the Natural History Museum in London.

Diving

In 1943 underwater exploration was revolutionized by the invention of the scuba (self-contained underwater breathing apparatus). The apparatus, patented as the Aqua-Lung by its inventors, Jacques-Yves Cousteau and Émile Gagnan, allows divers to swim freely to depths of 330 feet (100 m) and more with air cylinders on their back.

The Aqua-Lung has made the underwater world readily accessible. Of particular interest to divers are the coral reefs, ecosystems as biologically diverse as any tropical forest on

Below **Researchers from the Woods Hole Marine Biology Laboratory in Massachusetts collect marine organisms that are used to increase understanding of human biology. Founded in 1888, Woods Hole is the world's largest marine laboratory.**

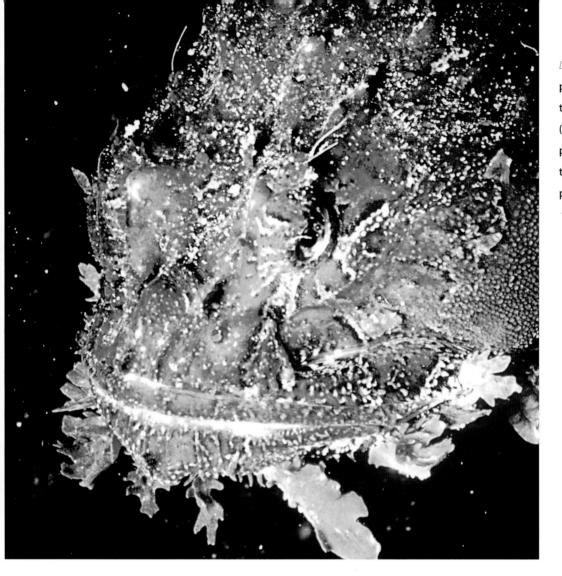

Breathing Underwater

*A*t sea level air pressure is equal to one bar. Being much denser than air, water exerts rapid increases of pressure with increased depth. The increase in pressure is one bar for every thirty-three feet (10 m) of depth. So if a diver tries to breathe through a pipe at a depth of only 3.3 feet (1 m), his or her lungs are already trying to expand against a pressure of 1.1 bar. Most people are unlikely to be able to fill their lungs sufficiently to survive for more than a few minutes at even such a shallow depth. In order to breathe at any greater depth, divers need to be supplied with air at a pressure that is equal to the pressure of the water they are swimming in.

There is an added complication. Divers are generally supplied with normal air, which contains a high concentration of nitrogen. Under pressure, nitrogen is absorbed by the blood. If the diver returns to the surface too quickly, the nitrogen is released too quickly; gas bubbles form in body tissue and cause a form of decompression sickness known as the bends, which can be fatal.

land that thrive in the shallow sunlit seas of the tropics. Particularly sensitive to changes in sea temperature, coral reefs are also important indicators of climate change. Through Reefcheck and other such organizations, networks of amateur divers provide a continuous record of coral reef data.

Most divers rarely swim deeper than one hundred feet (33 m). At greater depths a diver needs to breathe a special blend of oxygen, helium, and nitrogen in proportions different from those in normal air, in order to avoid decompression sickness (a condition that is also known as the bends). In 1979 the American undersea explorer Sylvia Earle experimented with a pressurized armored diving suit, called JIM. Earle reached the unprecedented depth of 1,250 feet (381 m) off the coast of Hawaii.

Above **This 1979 map of the world's ocean floors was compiled from millions of depth soundings taken using conventional and sonar techniques.**

Mapping the Seabed

The seabed is mapped by sonar devices, first developed during World War I to detect submarines. In 1923 the sonic depth finder, invented at the U.S. Naval Experimental Station in Annapolis, Maryland, produced a bathymetric map (a map that profiles the shape of the ocean floor).

GLORIA, a twenty-six-foot (8 m) side-scanning sonar device that is towed behind a ship, is capable of mapping an area of the seabed measuring 7,722 square miles (20,000 km²) in a single day. From 1984 to 1991 GLORIA mapped U.S. coastal waters in order to identify the location of important deposits of minerals and fish and in the process found many previously uncharted features.

With continuing improvements in technology, especially in the field of robotics, some researchers argue that taking people down into the deepest oceans is no longer worth the risk or the expense.

1661
Robert Boyle proposes a systematic exploration of the world's oceans.

1725
Luigi Ferdinando Marsili publishes *Histoire physique de la mer* (Physical history of the sea).

1795
The British Royal Navy forms the Hydrographic Office.

1856–1857
The route of the transatlantic telegraph is surveyed.

1872–1876
HMS *Challenger* circumnavigates the world and collects an unprecedented quantity of oceanographic data.

1943
Jacques-Yves Cousteau and Émile Gagnan invent the Aqua-Lung.

1978
NASA's *Seasat* satellite maps the ocean surface.

1984–1991
The GLORIA sonar device maps U.S. coastal waters.

1990–2002
The World Ocean Circulation Experiment uses satellite imagery and data collected by thirty nations in four oceans.

Observing the Oceans from Space

In addition to seagoing research vessels, modern oceanographers use satellites to observe the oceans from space. A satellite can map a much vaster area than would be possible with ships alone and thus provides a global view of the oceans as a single interrelated system. Satellites are mounted with sensors that measure changes in the height of the sea and identify pollutants and phytoplankton (masses of drifting plant life) to give an overall picture of the health of the oceans.

Underwater exploration is revealing an extraordinary new world. Among recent discoveries are an undersea landscape with a mountain range 40,000 miles (60,000 kms) long encircling the earth and canyons deeper than Mount Everest is high. In 2003 a smoking underwater volcano was found 9,843 feet (3,000 m) beneath the Indian Ocean on the Carlsberg Ridge. More than half of the world's oceans are over one mile deep, and it seems certain that many more exciting discoveries lie ahead.

Undersea Observatories

Jacques-Yves Cousteau (1910–1997) built the first live-in undersea observatories, named Continental Shelf (or Conshelf) Stations. Conshelf I housed two divers for seven days in thirty-three feet (10 m) of water beneath the Mediterranean Sea. The following year, Conshelf II housed eight divers under the Red Sea, and in Conshelf III scientists lived for a month in 197 feet (60 m) of water off the coast of France.

In 1969, in the belief that undersea conditions resemble those in space, NASA funded a project to build a kind of oceanic space station. The Caribbean Hydrolab, built by the U.S. National Oceanic and Atmospheric Administration (NOAA), provided a research base for over six hundred scientists between 1972 and 1985. NOAA now owns Aquarius, located at a depth of sixty-three feet (19.2 m) off the Florida Keys, where divers study the nearby coral reefs.

Left **Underwater divers at work outside Hydrolab in the Bahamas.**

SEE ALSO

- Cousteau, Jacques-Yves
- Satellites
- Ships and Boats
- Submersibles
- Tides and Currents

VANCOUVER, GEORGE

FROM 1791 TO 1795, GEORGE VANCOUVER, a British Royal Navy officer (1757–1798) commanded an expedition to map the western coast of North America between 30 and 60° north latitude. Vancouver covered 80,000 miles (129,000 km) in four and a half years and drew maps to new standards of accuracy. Yet powerful enemies in London saw to it that, during his lifetime, Vancouver did not receive the credit he deserved.

Below **The name Vancouver was given to a major Canadian island in honor of the explorer who sailed around it in 1792.**

IN THE SOUTH PACIFIC

George Vancouver was born in King's Lynn, a port in eastern England. At age fourteen he joined the Royal Navy as a midshipman (trainee officer). The following year he sailed aboard HMS *Resolution* on James Cook's second Pacific voyage (1772–1775). He proved his mettle in the cold seas near Antarctica by climbing out onto the *Resolution*'s bowsprit (a spar projecting from the front of the ship) so that he could claim to be the closest person to the South Pole. In recognition of Vancouver's abilities, Cook selected him for his third Pacific expedition (1776–1780), aboard the *Discovery*. Afterward Vancouver served in the Caribbean for a decade. He was made a commander in 1790.

VANCOUVER'S AMERICAN VOYAGE

The purpose of Cook's third Pacific voyage had been to locate a northwest passage joining the Pacific and Atlantic Oceans around or across North America. In April 1791 Vancouver sailed from Falmouth, in south-western England, with orders to continue the search. He was also ordered to reach a peaceful agreement with the Spanish in the area of Nootka Sound, a harbor on the western coast of present-day Vancouver Island. In 1785 British and Spanish traders had clashed over who had rights to the local waters, which were rich in sea otters and whales.

Vancouver's flagship, a new HMS *Discovery*, was accompanied by HMS *Chatham*, commanded by Lieutenant Broughton, and HMS *Daedalus*, a supply ship. Having sailed by way of southern Africa, Vancouver conducted preliminary surveys along the coasts of Australia and New Zealand before crossing the Pacific. In April 1792 the ships arrived at Cape Cabrillo, near present-day San Diego Bay.

VANCOUVER'S ACHIEVEMENT

At sea for over four and a half years, Vancouver circumnavigated the globe and lost only 6 of his crew of 150. The survival of his men was due in large part to the care that Vancouver took to prevent scurvy. He supplied his men with foods rich in vitamin C, such as oranges and spruce beer. He proved that the territory now known as Vancouver Island was in fact an island. Several places on the western coast of North America still bear names that Vancouver gave them, including

Charting the Coast

Vancouver was an extremely thorough navigator and surveyor. He took eighty-five lunar observations in order to be certain of his initial starting point on the California coast. Working slowly and methodically, he covered less than five miles per day. In order to map coastal inlets accurately, he sent teams along the shoreline in rowing boats. By the end of the voyage, Vancouver's teams had rowed approximately ten thousand miles (16,000 km). By the summer of 1795, Vancouver had charted the coast from California to Alaska and had produced the most accurate maps of the area ever drawn. In August he finally decided to return south. He named the place in present-day Alaska where he finished surveying Port Conclusion.

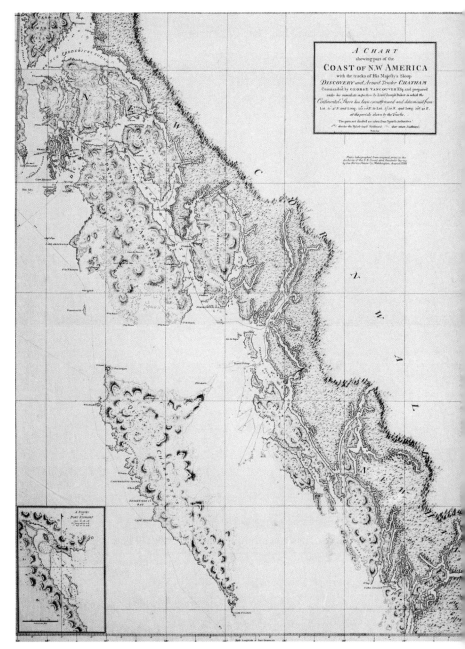

Above **This remarkably detailed map, which shows part of the coast of present-day British Columbia near Queen Charlotte Island, was drawn during Vancouver's painstaking survey of the Pacific Northwest.**

Mount Baker, Puget Sound, Port Discovery, and Hood Canal. Vancouver proved that there was no Northwest Passage south of 65° north latitude but was less successful in negotiating with the Spanish at Nootka Sound. In spite of Vancouver's efforts, the Spanish refused to leave the area.

Below **Cook's *Resolution* at anchor in Nootka Sound, Vancouver Island, in 1788. Local people offered to trade otter pelts, and Vancouver returned in 1792 to negotiate trading rights.**

Spruce Beer

During the seventeenth and eighteenth centuries, scurvy, the explorer's deadliest enemy, regularly decimated maritime crews. As early as 1535, Jacques Cartier and other European explorers of North America had learned from native peoples a recipe for boiling the leaves and twigs of black spruce (a tree of the pine family) with sugar, molasses, and honey and fermenting the mixture with yeast. The resulting concoction, known as spruce beer, proved extremely effective at preventing scurvy. Archibald Menzies, the surgeon and botanist on Vancouver's American voyage, advocated the use of spruce beer. By ensuring regular supplies for his crew, Vancouver kept the death toll from scurvy remarkably low.

FINAL YEARS

Vancouver's health was broken by the voyage, and on returning to Britain, he retired from the navy. He was not without his detractors; he had angered Joseph Banks, the leading scientist of the day, by trying to court-martial the voyage's botanist, Archibald Menzies. He had also disciplined a troublesome young officer who came from an aristocratic family. The officer disliked Vancouver and later challenged him to a duel. Vancouver managed to publish half of his voyage diaries before dying in 1798, only forty-one years of age.

1757
George Vancouver is born in England.

1771
Joins the Royal Navy.

1772–1780
Serves as a midshipman on James Cook's second and third Pacific voyages.

1791
Sets out on voyage to map the western coast of North America.

1792
Begins surveying 110 miles (177 km) north of San Francisco; negotiates with the Spanish at Nootka Sound.

1794
Completes his survey of North America's Pacific coast at Port Conclusion and returns south.

1795
Returns to England via Cape Horn.

1798
Dies at the age of forty-one.

SEE ALSO

- Banks, Joseph
- Cook, James
- Illness and Disease
- Northwest Passage

VERRAZZANO, GIOVANNI DA

COMMISSIONED BY KING FRANCIS I OF FRANCE to locate a passage from the Atlantic to the Pacific through North America, the Italian navigator and explorer Giovanni da Verrazzano (c. 1485–c. 1528) sailed from present-day North Carolina to Newfoundland. His voyage proved that North America had a continuous eastern coastline, and he became the first European to enter New York Bay.

Below **This seventeenth-century ceramic bust is purported to represent Giovanni da Verrazzano.**

Giovanni da Verrazzano was born into a wealthy family in the Castle of Verrazzano, on a hilltop overlooking the Greve valley, a wine-producing area thirty miles south of Florence, in central Italy. After receiving a classical education, Verrazzano moved to Lyons, in eastern France. Little is known about his early life, but it is believed that he learned the art of sailing during voyages around the Mediterranean Sea. He is also thought to have visited the Middle East and Newfoundland (the eastern extremity of present-day Canada).

THE NEW WORLD
During his youth in Italy, Verrazzano would undoubtedly have heard about the voyages of his compatriot Christopher Columbus, who in 1492 became the first European to visit the Americas, a previously unknown continent. Though many European explorers sailed to the New World in Columbus's wake, their efforts were concentrated on the Caribbean and Central America, and North America was relatively unexplored. In 1497 the Italian explorer John Cabot had sailed to Newfoundland, and in 1513 Juan Ponce de León led a Spanish expedition to Florida, but in the 1520s little was known about the two thousand miles of coastline in between. Most enticing of all was the possibility of a short passage connecting the Atlantic and Pacific Oceans, which would afford a direct route from Europe to the riches of Asia.

Quinfay

Archipelagus 7448 infularu

Zipangu

pdonum

FRANCISCA
C. Britonum

Terra florida

Oceanus occider

Chamaho

Panuco Inf. Tonucaru

Tenuidma

CVBA

Hifpaniola

Antilæ

Sciluz

Tlmiftitan

Coxumella

S. Paul

Iamica

Dominica

Catigara

Neragua

PARIAS abundat auro & margaritis

Canibali

Nouus   orbis

Infula Atlantica quam no-
cant Brafilu & Americam.

Die Nüw

Inf. infortu nacæ

Welt

Regio Gigantum

Calenfuan

7.infule
gueri

Mate pacificum

Eretum Magalinni

Above **Sebastian Munster's *Cosmographia Universalis* (1550) reflected the widespread European belief in a narrow North America.**

In 1522 Verrazzano asked King Francis I of France to finance an expedition to North America. Although the French had yet to sponsor a New World voyage, Francis I apparently perceived the great advantage of establishing a presence in the Americas and of perhaps finding a route to the Pacific. He supplied Verrazzano with a royal ship, *La Dauphine,* and enough provisions to last eight months.

CROSSING THE ATLANTIC

Verrazzano sailed with four ships from Dieppe, in northern France, in January 1524. Among the company was Girolamo da Verrazzano, Giovanni's younger brother. Soon after departure two of the ships were wrecked, and a third turned back. After a stop at the Portuguese island of Madeira, *La Dauphine* set sail alone across the Atlantic. Having survived a terrible storm, Verrazzano

Girolamo da Verrazzano

*I*n 1529, a few years after his brother's death, Girolamo da Verrazzano produced a map of the world incorporating the information he had gathered on the North American voyage. Although Girolamo's map was accurate in its depiction of a continuous coastline from Florida to Newfoundland, it promulgated his brother's belief that, in the area of present-day South Carolina, a narrow isthmus of land separated the Atlantic from the Pacific. Girolamo used the names his brother had chosen for the North American territories, including Francesca (deriving almost certainly from the name of the French king) and Nova Gallia (New Gaul, from the Roman name for France).

finally sighted land on March 20, 1524. Five days later he found a safe harbor and was able to come ashore at what is probably present-day Cape Fear, in southern North Carolina.

EXPLORING THE EAST COAST OF AMERICA

Verrazzano soon found himself surrounded by Native Americans, who welcomed the Europeans and offered them food. When Verrazzano explored a short way inland, he was impressed by the landscape and the lush vegetation he saw. In a letter he later wrote to King Francis I, he described a land "as pleasant and delectable to behold, as is possible to imagine."

Continuing northward, Verrazzano saw to the west, beyond a narrow strip of land, a stretch of open water. He recorded in his log his excitement at finding a sea that might lead to the "happy shores of Cathay [China]." In fact, the Pamlico Sound merely separates a ribbon of sandy islands, known as the Carolina Outer Banks, from the mainland. Nevertheless, Verrazzano's optimism was reflected on the 1529 map drawn by his brother, which has an extremely narrow North America bounded to the west by the Sea of Verrazzano. The error, which suggested an easy passage from the Atlantic to the Pacific, was copied by mapmakers for over a century.

NEW YORK

In mid-April Verrazzano became the first European to lay eyes on New York Bay. Once again, local Native Americans treated the strangers well; in Verrazzano's words, "they came towards us very cheerfully, making great shouts of admiration." Verrazzano continued north along Long Island Sound to Block Island, southwest of present-day Rhode Island. He compared the area to the Greek island of Rhodes and wrote colorful descriptions of the local people.

c. 1485	**JANUARY 1524**	**APRIL 1524**	**1528**	**1529**
Giovanni da Verrazzano is born in Greve, Italy.	Departs Dieppe.	Reaches New York Bay.	On his third expedition, lands in Florida, explores the Lesser Antilles, and is captured and eaten by cannibals.	Girolamo da Verrazzano publishes a map of the world.
1522 Asks King Francis I to finance a voyage to the New World.	**MARCH 1524** Lands in America, probably at or near Cape Fear, in North Carolina.	**JULY 1524** Arrives back in Dieppe. **1526** On his second expedition, lands in Brazil.		

Verrazzano continued east to present-day Narragansett Bay, where the welcome he received from the local Wampanoag Indians was so warm that he broke with custom and anchored near the coast. He was shown a better harbor, near present-day Newport, Rhode Island, and spent two weeks there trading and waiting for better weather. He then continued through the Vineyard and Nantucket Sounds, around Cape Cod, and eastward to the coast of present-day Maine, where the local people were not so welcoming as those he had previously encountered. He wrote of their "evil manners, so barbarous, that despite all the signs we could make, we could never converse with them."

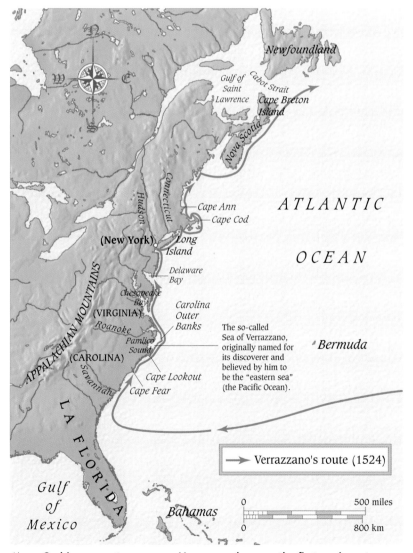

Above **On his momentous voyage Verrazzano became the first explorer to name discoveries in the New World after people and places in the Old.**

Verrazzano gave a detailed description of the people who greeted him at Block Island:

The things that they esteem most of all those which we gave them, were bells, crystal of azure color, and other toys to hang at their ears or about their necks. They did not desire cloth of silk or of gold . . . neither cared they for things made of steel and iron which we often showed them in our armor which they made no wonder at, and in beholding them they only asked the art of making them like they did our glasses, which when they beheld, they suddenly laughed.

From a letter to King Francis I, written in Dieppe in July 1524

On the final leg of his journey, Verrazzano reached Newfoundland. He did not see the Cabot Strait, which separates Newfoundland from Nova Scotia, and therefore believed that Newfoundland was continuous with the North American mainland. As Newfoundland was in Portuguese hands, Verrazzano did not stop but sailed directly back to France and arrived in Dieppe on July 8, 1524.

GRISLY END

Verrazzano made two further expeditions to the Americas. In 1526 he reached Brazil, and in 1528 he traveled to Florida and explored the Lesser Antilles, islands in the southern Caribbean. He was captured by cannibals, possibly on the island of Guadeloupe. Girolamo watched in horror as his brother was killed and his flesh eaten.

SEE ALSO

- Cabot, John • Cartier, Jacques
- Columbus, Christopher • France

VESPUCCI, AMERIGO

AMERIGO VESPUCCI (1454–1512) has been immortalized as the explorer from whose name America is derived. An Italian who sailed for the Spanish and the Portuguese, Vespucci left little in the way of a reliable account of his voyages. Perhaps his greatest achievement was to recognize, on the second of the two New World voyages he indisputably made, that South America was not part of or adjacent to Asia but a previously unknown continental landmass.

Below **In this contemporary portrait, Vespucci is depicted using the tools of a navigator.**

AMERICUS VESPUTIUS

Amerigo Vespucci was born in Florence, Italy, into a family of rich merchants. For many years he continued the family tradition by working as a merchant for the Medicis, an extremely wealthy and influential Florentine family of bankers, statesmen, and patrons of the arts. Around 1495 Vespucci had his first taste of seafaring when he was employed by the Medicis to head one of their ship-outfitting businesses in Seville, in southwestern Spain.

VESPUCCI AND COLUMBUS

When Vespucci arrived in Seville, the Spanish were undertaking the first voyages of exploration west across the Atlantic. In 1492 and 1493 Christopher Columbus had explored the Caribbean, and on his third voyage, in 1498, he became the first European to land on the American mainland. Though previously believing he had managed to sail to Asia, on this third voyage Columbus, recognizing (at least in part) the nature of the lands he visited, wrote, "this is another world [*otro mundo*], hitherto unknown." (His error lay in believing that the New World was adjacent to or even an outlying part of Asia). During this period, it seems that Vespucci and Columbus became personally acquainted; the company of ship outfitters that employed Vespucci helped prepare Columbus's ships for his voyage of 1498.

ACROSS THE ATLANTIC

In 1499 Vespucci served as astronomer and navigator under the captainship of Alonso de Ojeda (c. 1458–c. 1516), who had sailed with Columbus in 1493. Four ships left the port of Santa Maria, on the Gulf of Cadiz in southwestern Spain. Upon arrival in present-day Venezuela, Vespucci left Ojeda and detoured southward, in the process becoming the first European to see the mouth of the Amazon River. In the belief that he was skirting the easternmost coast of Asia, he named the Amazon's mouth the Gulf of the Ganges (a river in India). A short while later Vespucci returned northward. He arrived back in Cadiz in September 1500.

Below **This illustration of Vespucci navigating by the stars using a mariner's astrolabe decorates a French manuscript.**

NEW WORLD

The following year Vespucci made a journey to South America under the Portuguese flag. On May 14, 1501, three ships set sail from Lisbon, the Portuguese capital, and crossed to South America via the Cape Verde Islands. Once again Vespucci explored the coast of Brazil; he made a fundamental contribution to the history of exploration when he declared his conviction that the land he was exploring was a new continent, entirely distinct from Asia.

In September 1504 Vespucci wrote a letter describing his travels, which was published, together with two Latin versions of the same letter, in Florence in 1505. His description of

Vespucci claimed to have encountered native South Americans on a voyage of 1497:

. . . they go entirely naked, as well the men as the women. . . . They are of medium stature, very well proportioned: their flesh is of a colour the verges into red like a lion's mane . . . they have not any hair upon the body, except the hair of the head which is long and black, and especially in the women, whom it renders handsome . . . they let no hair grow on their eyebrows, nor on their eyelids, nor elsewhere, except the hair of the head: for they hold hairiness to be a filthy thing . . .

Letter to Pier Soderini, gonfalonier of the Republic of Florence (1504)

the "new world" (*mundus novus*) he had visited and the warm reception he had received from its inhabitants generated a great deal of excitment.

How Many Voyages Did Vespucci Make?

In his account of his travels, Vespucci is vague on geographical detail and, it is thought, exaggerates his own achievement. He claims to have made an earlier voyage to the New World in 1497, when he was in his mid-forties. According to his account, he sailed to Brazil, crossed the Gulf of Mexico, and traveled up the Atlantic coast of North America as far as the Gulf of Saint Lawrence, in present-day Canada. Beyond Vespucci's letter, there is little reliable evidence of this expedition, and most historians consider it unlikely that such a voyage ever took place. Vespucci may have wanted to preempt Coumbus (who reached the American mainland in 1498) and be credited as the discoverer of the new continent. The 1499 voyage with Ojeda is generally treated as Vespucci's first.

Below **Knowledge of the eastern coast of South America increased rapidly after Vespucci's voyage of 1499. Owing to the unreliability of his accounts, however, Vespucci's precise route is uncertain.**

August 17,1501: Vespucci makes landfall near Cabo São Roque.

"I believe these two rivers, by reason of their enormous size, create the freshwater area in the ocean." (Vespucci)

August 23,1501: Vespucci anchors off Cabo Santo Agostinho.

The southward reach of Vespucci's 1501–1502 voyage is uncertain. Although his claim to have reached 50°S is unlikely to be true, Vespucci's statement that he "navigated in the Southern hemisphere for nine months and twenty-seven days" may well be accurate.

"We found so many different animals that I believe so many species could not have entered Noah's Ark." (Vespucci)

January 1,1502: Vespucci enters Guanabara Bay.

→ 1499
→ 1501–1502

1454	1497	1501–1502	1507	1512
Amerigo Vespucci is born in Florence.	Perhaps makes a voyage to the Americas.	Makes his second voyage to South America.	The German cartographer Martin Waldseemüller produces the first map to use the name America.	Vespucci dies of malaria in Spain.
c. 1495 Moves to Seville.	**1499** Makes his first fully documented voyage to South America.	**1503** Possibly makes a final voyage to South America.		

Right **By the time he produced this map of the world in 1513, Martin Waldseemüller had revised his previously high opinion of Vespucci and declared that the greatest pioneer of New World discovery was Christopher Columbus. Nevertheless, the name America stuck.**

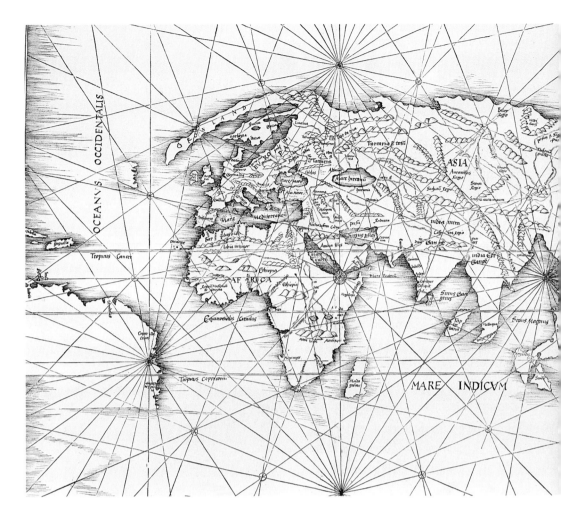

FINAL YEARS

Although Vespucci claimed to have made a fourth voyage to the Americas in 1503, his report has never been satisfactorily verified. According to his account, he sailed southward along the Atlantic coast of South America in an attempt to determine the size of the new continent. He ventured as far as the mouth of the Plate River (Río de la Plata), on the border of present-day Argentina and Uruguay, and returned to Spain in June 1504.

In 1505 Vespucci was hired by the Casa de las Indias (House of the Indies) in Seville and in 1508 was appointed chief examiner of pilots, a post of considerable prestige and responsibility. His tasks was to check the reports of pilots traveling to the Americas and to assimilate all the data furnished by such voyages into the official Spanish royal map of the New World territories. He held this position until his death in 1512 from malaria.

Naming America

*I*n 1507 the German cartographer Martin Waldseemüller reprinted *Quattuor Americi navigationes* (Four voyages of Amerigo), a Latin version of the letter written by Vespucci in 1504. Together with the letter Waldseemüller printed a pamphlet of his own entitled *Cosmographiae introductio* (Introduction to cosmography), which included a map of the world on twelve sheets. He suggested that the newly discovered world be named "ab Americo Inventore" ("after Amerigo the discoverer") and used the name America (though applied only to South America) for the first time. In 1513 Waldseemüller revised his assessment of Vespucci, but by then it was too late—the name America had come to stay.

SEE ALSO

- Columbus, Christopher • Mapmaking
- Portugal • Spain

VIKINGS

ALTHOUGH NUMBERING SCARCELY TWO MILLION at their peak, the Vikings of Scandinavia had a significant and lasting impact on the world. Between around 800 and 1100 Viking armies terrorized much of northern Europe with both snatch-and-grab raids of coastal regions and long-term programs of conquest and settlement. Notable explorers as well as fearsome warriors, the Vikings influenced an area extending from Baghdad and Constantinople in the east to Iceland, Greenland, and North America in the west.

WHO WERE THE VIKINGS?

The Vikings, also known as Norsemen, lived in Scandinavia, a region of northern Europe that includes the present-day countries of Denmark, Norway, and Sweden. The same ethnic (if not political) boundaries prevailed then as now—Danes, Swedes, and Norwegians formed three distinct groups among the Vikings. Nonetheless, the Vikings shared a language, a religion, and many customs and traditions. The word Viking itself is derived from a Scandinavian word meaning "pirate."

WHAT SPARKED VIKING EXPANSION?

Scandinavian society was divided into three classes: nobles, freemen, and slaves. However, the status of freemen differed from that of freemen in other parts of Europe. Elsewhere, feudal obligations to local lords restricted the freedom and movement of the people who fell within this class. In Scandinavia, on the other hand, a freeman was at liberty to increase his wealth and standing by leaving his town or village to raid or settle in other territories. Owing to an increasing population and a short supply of Scandinavian farmland, many freemen were pressured to venture away from home. Inevitably, some chose to venture overseas. They were able to do so because of the remarkable sophistication of Scandinavian shipbuilding. Viking vessels, both speedy and sturdy, were among the finest seagoing vessels of their era.

Below **Ales Stenar (Stones of Ale), a monumental formation of fifty-nine stones laid out in the shape of a longship 220 feet (67 m) long and 62 feet (19 m) wide, is located on the southern coast of Sweden.**

Above This illustration of a Viking warship, with a figurehead in the form of a mythical beast and a sail wrapped around the mast, is taken from an Anglo-Saxon manuscript that dates from around 1050.

750–800
Swedish Vikings begin to establish trading links with territories to the east and south.

793
Viking raids on English monasteries begin.

800
Swedish Vikings begin to explore Russia.

840
Norwegian Vikings establish a settlement at Dublin.

860
Norwegian Vikings begin to colonize Iceland.

982
Erik the Red discovers Greenland.

Viking Ships

From the late eighth century Scandinavian shipbuilders made a number of improvements to their oar-driven ships. Tall masts enabled the deployment of large, square woolen sails. To support these masts and sails, stronger and more stable keels were developed. The end result was a long, low boat with a high, curving prow (at the front) and stern (at the rear). With a structure pared down to a lightweight minimum, Viking ships were both fast and maneuverable. However, they were also sturdy enough to undertake long voyages over open (and often choppy) water. With their shallow draft they were easy to beach on a sandy shore or sail inland up a river.

The Vikings expressed their pride in their boats with finely detailed decorations. Some had gilded wind vanes at their prow, engraved with elaborate depictions of mythical beasts. Others had distinctive figureheads, often in fierce designs, such as a snarling dragon. The arrival of a Viking fleet struck fear into the hearts of any whose territory the Vikings invaded.

All Scandinavian countries have an extensive coastline. Inland, much of Scandinavia is mountainous and inhospitable, so Viking settlements tended to accumulate in coastal regions. Born seafarers, the Scandinavians had plenty of opportunity to test their navigational skill along local shores.

VIKING MIGRATIONS

Broadly speaking, Danish, Swedish, and Norwegian Vikings expanded in different directions depending on their geographical position within Scandinavia. Occasionally, however, their paths crossed. On many such occasions they fought savage battles with each other for control of disputed territory.

The Danes, who lived farthest south, raided and settled in England, France, and Spain and traveled into the Mediterranean as far as Sicily. The Swedes, whose homeland was in eastern Scandinavia, explored the Baltic Sea and from there made inland journeys along the waterways of eastern Europe and Russia. They traveled as far south as Constantinople (present-day Istanbul, in Turkey), where Viking warriors formed an elite body of troops known as the Varagian Guard. Swedish Vikings even traveled to Baghdad (in Iraq). Where

travel by boat was not possible, routes were explored on foot, on skis, on horseback, and even by camel.

The Norwegians, who inhabited western Scandinavia, were perhaps the most daring of Viking explorers. They raided the coasts of northern England, Scotland, the outlying Scottish Islands, and Ireland, where they founded the present-day Irish capital of Dublin.

Venturing farther north and west across the North Atlantic, Norwegian Vikings settled the isolated Faeroe Islands. On one trip to those islands, a boat blown off course made the accidental discovery of Iceland. Such was the demand for new farmland that within a century tens of thousands of Norwegians made the perilous six-day, seven-hundred-mile (1,130 km) journey to this bleak outpost. By the late tenth century the Norse colony on Iceland was 60,000 strong. When Iceland's limited supply of good farmland had been claimed, Norwegian Vikings ventured 450 miles (725 km) farther west to Greenland, which was probably given that name by the pioneer colonist Erik the Red to make the ice-covered land sound more attractive to potential settlers than it really was.

986
The colonization of Greenland begins.

1001
Leif Eriksson lands in North America.

Above **This Viking burial site is located at Lindholm Hoje, near Ålborg, in northern Denmark.**

Until recently, Viking sagas telling of visits to North America were discounted as myths. However, fresh archaeological evidence of a substantial Viking settlement at L'Anse aux Meadows, in Newfoundland, seems to prove the truth of the sagas.

THE END OF AN ERA

For some three hundred years, the Vikings were Europe's most accomplished warriors and explorers. The era of their dominance came to an end with the rise of the Normans, themselves descended from the Norsemen who had settled in the north of France. Ultimately, the Vikings were too few in number to establish a lasting dominion over the vast tracts of territory where they made their influence felt. More often than not, rather than rule as a conquering power, Viking settlers assimilated with local populations. By 1100 Viking settlements throughout Europe had begun to lose their distinctively Scandinavian character.

From Greenland Erik's son, Leif Eriksson, made a daring voyage to Newfoundland, in North America. He and his crew were the first Europeans to land on the American continent, an achievement that predated Christopher Columbus by five hundred years.

SEE ALSO

- Erik the Red • Gudrid • Leif Eriksson
- Scandinavia

WALLACE, ALFRED RUSSEL

AFTER SEVERAL YEARS spent collecting specimens of animal and plant life, first in South America and later in Southeast Asia, the Welsh-born naturalist Alfred Russel Wallace (1823–1913) developed theories about the origin and development of species. Although Wallace worked independently of Charles Darwin, the two men drew similar conclusions about evolution; indeed, Wallace's writings were a major influence on Darwin. By the end of his life, Wallace was one of the most celebrated writers and thinkers of his era.

Below **Alfred Russel Wallace, probably the most famous British scientific writer of the late nineteenth century, published books well into his eighties.**

Alfred Russel Wallace was born at Usk, in southeastern Wales, in 1823. His early education was hampered by his own poor health and by his family's financial difficulties. At age fourteen, Alfred Wallace became an apprentice to his eldest brother, William, who was a surveyor. Under the tutelage of his brother, Alfred learned a range of practical skills, including mapmaking, mathematics, mechanics, chemistry, and construction. He went on to spend two years as a teacher of drafting, surveying, English, and arithmetic in Leicester, in central England.

While in Leicester, Wallace became friendly with a young naturalist, Henry Walter Bates (1825–1892). Though two years younger than Wallace, Bates had already established himself as an accomplished entomologist (a collector and studier of insects). Wallace developed a keen interest in Bates's collecting activities, and before long the two men came to realize that they shared a common passion for the natural sciences.

The possibility of combining the study of the natural world with travel to exotic regions was suggested to Wallace in 1847, when he read a new book by William Henry Edwards entitled *A Voyage up the River Amazon*. In 1848 Wallace and Bates decided to travel to the Amazon basin themselves to gather biological specimens.

Above **Henry Walter Bates (1825–1892), an entomologist who shared Wallace's interests, traveled to South America with Wallace in 1848. He returned to England in 1859 from the Amazon with a collection of 14,000 specimens.**

COLLECTING SPECIMENS

In May 1848 Wallace and Bates landed at Pará (present-day Belém), in northern Brazil. They traveled together for over a year and then separated, in order that between them they might cover a larger area. Wallace spent four years in the middle Amazon region. Focusing his studies on the geographical distribution of different species and different members within the same species, he investigated the area's birds, insects, primates, fish, plants, and physical geography. He also spent much time studying the customs and language of the native peoples he worked among.

In 1852 ill health prevented Wallace from continuing his studies, and he began the long journey back to Pará. From there he set sail for Britain, but on August 6 his ship, carrying his precious specimens, caught fire and sank to the bottom of the ocean. Wallace spent ten days in a leaking lifeboat and was fortunate to be saved by a passing cargo ship.

SURVIVAL OF THE FITTEST

While Wallace had learned much in South America, his studies had not produced the definitive conclusions he had hoped for about the exact nature and process of evolution. He decided to continue collecting, and in 1854, with the help of London's Royal Geographical Society, he traveled to the Malay Archipelago (present-day Indonesia). This expedition was described in his 1869 study, *Malay Archipelago*.

Wallace spent eight years in Indonesia and during over seventy separate expeditions

Wallace's Line

During his travels through the Malay Archipelago, Wallace noted that animal and plant life in the area was divided along a hypothetical line that runs between Asia and Australia. Wallace's Line, as it became known, divides the islands of Bali from Lombok and Borneo from Sulawesi. Species to the west of this line are mostly Asiatic, while those to the east are of Australasian origin. After Wallace's death, geologists realized that Wallace's Line was also a boundary between two tectonic plates (separate parts of the earth's crust).

covered more than 14,000 miles (22,530 km). He collected more than 125,000 specimens, an astonishing total of which more than a thousand were members of species previously unknown to science.

In February 1858 Wallace fell ill with malaria and was confined to bed. This period of enforced inactivity gave Wallace a chance to think more deeply about the way in which species adapt over time. He had read the ideas of the English economist Thomas Malthus (1766–1834), who believed that famine and disease act as a natural check on human populations. Applying this idea to changes in the natural world, Wallace developed the idea of evolution by natural selection. According to this process, also known as "survival of the fittest," the members of a species that are best suited to survive in their environment are more likely to live long enough to reproduce. They pass on their genetic makeup to their offspring, and so the species as a whole gradually evolves to fit its environment.

JANUARY 8, 1823
Alfred Russel Wallace is born in Wales.

APRIL 1848
Travels to South America.

OCTOBER 1852
Returns to Britain after being shipwrecked in the Atlantic.

1854
Begins collecting specimens in the Malay Archipelago.

1855
First writes down his ideas on evolution.

1858
Shares his ideas with Charles Darwin.

1869
Malay Archipelago is published.

1870
With Darwin, publishes works on evolution by natural selection.

NOVEMBER 7, 1913
Dies at his home in Dorset, in southwestern England.

Above **Working quite separately from each other, both Wallace and Charles Darwin (pictured here) developed the same theory of evolution by natural selection.**

Wallace argued that the controversy that greeted the theory of evolution was inevitable:

Truth is born into this world only with pangs and tribulations, and every fresh truth is received unwillingly. To expect the world to receive a new truth, or even an old truth, without challenging it, is to look for one of those miracles which do not occur.

From an interview with W. B. Northrop, published in *The Outlook* (New York) in 1913.

debate that followed the publication in 1859 of his *Origin of Species*, which offended, among others, those who believed that the theory of natural selection ran counter to the teachings of Christianity.

A SOCIAL THINKER

During the latter part of the nineteenth century, Wallace elucidated the theory of natural selection in several important books. Perhaps mindful of the financial hardship that his family had suffered during his childhood, Wallace also campaigned for social justice and equality of opportunity. He took a particular interest in the ideas of the Welshman Robert Owen (1771–1858) and other socialists who hoped that their work would improve the life of people of the working class. In later life Wallace supported a variety of causes, including the campaign for women's suffrage (the extension of the right to vote to women) and the nationalization of land ownership. By the end of his life in 1913, Wallace was one of the world's most celebrated and honored scientists.

WALLACE AND DARWIN

Wallace formed his theory of evolution by natural selection at the very same time Charles Darwin was reaching the same conclusions. In a letter he wrote to Darwin from Indonesia, Wallace explained his theories, and on July 1, 1858, papers written by both men were read to the Linnean Society of London. Darwin gained greater fame (and no small measure of infamy) because of the public

SEE ALSO

• Darwin, Charles • Humboldt, Alexander von

WEATHER FORECASTING

THE DIFFERENCE BETWEEN good weather and bad weather can mean the difference between success and failure (and in many cases life and death) for an explorer. A sound understanding of weather has always been vital for explorers traveling in any terrain or at sea. Although the technology available to meteorologists (weather forecasters) improved dramatically during the twentieth century, the principles of weather forecasting—observation and prediction—are exactly those that originated far back in prehistory.

Below **Satellites can be used to track the direction and speed of storms. Hurricane Fran was photographed by the weather satellite** *GOES* **in 1996 shortly before it struck the eastern coast of the United States.**

WEATHER IN THE ANCIENT WORLD

Unsurprisingly, the earliest recorded academic studies of the weather were written by the ancient Greeks, a people whose habit of migration, colonization, and territorial expansion took them on long exploratory voyages. The physican Hippocrates (c. 460–c. 377 BCE), author of one of the earliest weather books, *Airs, Waters, and Places*, recognized the powerful effect worked by weather and climate upon people's health. Around the year 340 BCE, the Greek philosopher Aristotle attempted to explain the nature and causes of the entire range of atmospheric phenomena, including clouds, winds, lightning, rain, and snow, in his book *Meteorologica*. The title of Aristotle's work, which derived from the Greek word *meteoron* ("high in the air") gave the name *meteorology* to the modern science of weather forecasting.

MEDIEVAL WEATHERMEN

From around 790 to 1100 CE, Viking sailors undertook long sea voyages from Scandinavia across the rough North Atlantic toward the outlying Scottish islands and beyond to Iceland, Greenland, and even North America. Weather forecasting was an essential part of the planning of Viking voyages. At the top of their mast, most Viking ships carried a cloth pennant (called a *fani*, or vane) to indicate the strength and direction of the wind. Viking sailors wore sacred charms that were meant to win the favor of Thor, the god of thunder and storms.

According to an old Scottish rhyme, "if Candlemas Day is bright and clear, there'll be twa winters in the year." (Candlemas is a Christian festival that falls on February 2). According to an ancient German tradition, if a hedgehog emerging from hibernation on Candlemas casts a shadow (an indication that the sun is shining), six more weeks of winter weather will follow. During the nineteenth century German settlers brought this tradition to the United States in the form of Groundhog Day, celebrated on February 2 in Punxsutawney, Pennsylvania. According to the tradition, a groundhog will return to its burrow if, upon emerging on February 2, it casts a shadow (and conversely, if the day is cloudy, the groundhog takes it as a sign of spring and remains above ground).

Many such weather forecasting traditions have a basis in scientific fact. For example, the well-known rhyme "red sky at night, sailor's delight," can be verified; a red or pink color in the evening sky is often caused by sunlight shining upon dry dust particles in the air, usually a sign that dry, stable weather is ahead.

THE SCIENCE OF WEATHER

In the fifteenth century scientific weather forecasting instruments began to appear. The German philosopher and churchman Nicholas of Cusa (1401–1464) designed the first hygrometer, an instrument for measuring the humidity of air. In 1592 the Italian astronomer Galileo Galilei (1564–1642) designed an atmospheric thermometer, an instrument for measuring the temperature of air. In 1643 Galileo's protegé Evangelista Torricelli (1608–1647) invented a mercury barometer, an instrument for measuring atmospheric pressure. During the 1660s Ferdinand II de' Medici (1610–1670), the grand duke of Tuscany, set up the world's first weather observation network. The network

Above **In 1643 Evangelista Torricelli noted that mercury in a glass tube rose and fell as the atmopheric pressure changed. This discovery led to the invention of the barometer.**

Evidence of medieval weather forecasting survives in European folklore, particularly in simple rhymes that were easily memorized and passed from one generation to the next. The climatic conditions of certain days in the year were used as milestones to indicate future weather. In England, for example, rain on Saint Swithin's Day (July 15) was supposed to signal another forty days of wet weather.

The Tower of the Winds

In the first century BCE, the Greek astronomer Andronicus of Cyrrhus designed and built the Tower of the Winds in Athens. The octagonal marble tower held a water clock and eight sundials. Mounted on top was an eight-foot (2.4 m) weather vane in the shape of Triton, the merman (half man, half fish) demigod of the sea. In Triton's hand was a pointed wand that indicated the direction in which the wind was blowing.

encompassed the Italian cities of Florence, Pisa, Bologna, and Milan, as well as Paris (France), Innsbruck (Austria), and Warsaw (Poland). Twice a day observers at each location recorded the temperature, pressure, humidity, state of the sky, and force and direction of the wind.

In the nineteenth century the British navy played an important role in the development of weather forecasting. In 1805 Admiral Francis Beaufort (1774–1857) drew up a simple but effective scale for measuring wind strength, which he based on observations of the influence of the wind on trees, smoke, and water. The Beaufort scale ranged from calm, or zero strength, to a maximum of twelve, or hurricane level.

In the United States, Meriwether Lewis and William Clark noted daily weather conditions in their journals during their historic 1804 exploration of the West. In 1849 Professor Joseph Henry of the Smithsonian Institution established a national network of more than 150 weather observation stations connected via telegraph.

Left **The Tower of the Winds, the oldest surviving weather station, was built in Athens by the Greek astronomer Andronicus of Cyrrhus around 50 BCE.**

WEATHER FORECASTING IN THE AIR

In 1783 the French brothers Joseph-Michel and Jacques Étienne Montgolfier made the first manned ascent in a hot air balloon. Later the same year the French scientist Jacques Charles (1746–1823) took a balloon to a height of 8,860 feet (2,700 m), an altitude he measured with a barometer. After Charles's experiment, meteorologists realized that, by measuring the weather at high altitudes, they might produce accurate weather forecasts. The English scientist James Glaisher (1809–1903) reached a record altitude of over six miles (9,656 m) above sea level in a balloon. Glaisher attempted to take measurements of air temperature and humidity, but owing to the lower concentration of oxygen in the air at such an altitude, he passed out and almost suffocated.

In the early twentieth century meteorologists began to use aircraft to observe high-altitude weather patterns. During World War I (1914–1918) meteorologists flew high above the European battlefields and predicted the weather that the armies would imminently be subject to. Generals on both sides hoped for a dry forecast so that they could move their men more easily across the flat and easily flooded countryside of Belgium and northern France. After World War II (1939–1945), airborne radar arrays were used to track moving weather phenomena, such as hurricanes and tornadoes.

SATELLITES AND COMPUTERS

In the era of space exploration, it became possible for the first time to observe global weather from beyond the earth's atmosphere. In 1960 NASA launched the first of a series of worldwide weather observation satellites. TIROS (*t*elevision and *i*nfrared *o*bservation *s*atellite) was equipped with television cameras and infrared detectors that took pictures of the world's changing weather and

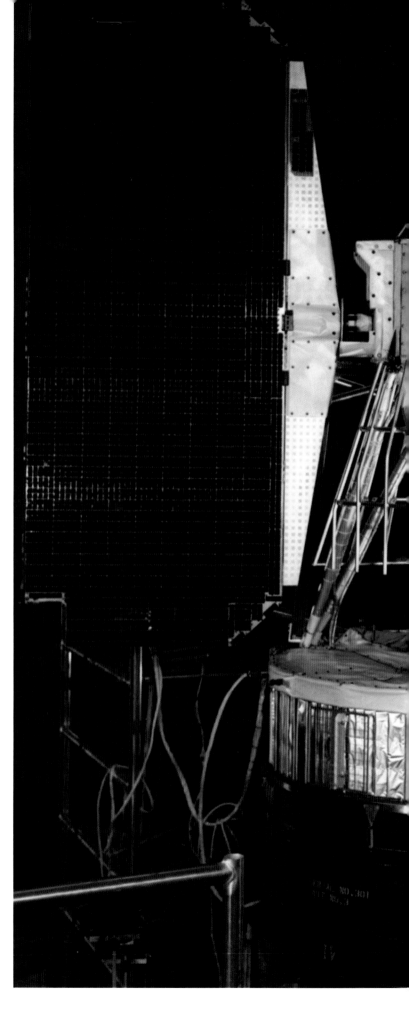

*L*uke Howard was born into an English Quaker family that valued education. In 1783, at age eleven, he saw a remarkable array of colors in the Oxfordshire sky. Having learned that the colorful display had been caused by massive volcanic eruptions in Iceland and Japan, he was inspired to study the phenomena of the earth's atmosphere.

In 1802 Howard gave a lecture in which he identified four basic types of clouds and gave them Latin names. The four clouds were cumulus (heaped), stratus (layered), cirrus (wispy), and nimbus (rain cloud). Howard believed that future weather might be forecast by studying clouds. He knew, for example, that if the skies were full of cumulus, stratus, or cirrus clouds, rain was unlikely. Howard's method of classifying clouds is still used by meteorologists.

Left Launched from Vandenberg Air Force Base, California, in August 1964, *Nimbus-A* was one of several pioneer geostationary satellites launched to collect information about weather systems.

transmitted them back to earth. By the end of the 1970s several geostationary satellites (those whose orbit keeps them above the same part of the earth) were sending back a vast amount of weather data. In the 1980s the development and improvement of high-speed computers enabled the data to be assimilated more efficiently, and before the end of the decade, weather patterns could be calculated with great precision.

SEE ALSO

- Aviation • Lewis and Clark Expedition
- Remote Sensing • Satellites
- Smithsonian Institution

WOMEN AND EXPLORATION

THROUGHOUT RECORDED HISTORY EXPLORATION has been largely, at times almost exclusively, a masculine affair. Of those explorers whose names are known to the public at large, the overwhelming majority are men. Nevertheless, quite a few women have been significant explorers—far more, in fact, than one might expect in light of the roles women have traditionally filled in virtually every society. As ever fewer societies continue to link specific spheres of activity with one sex or the other, the likelihood that future "household names" in exploration will be female ones continues to grow.

Right **The Dutch explorer and botanist Alexandrine-Pieternella-Françoise-Tinné traveled into the heart of Africa in the 1860s.**

WOMEN IN SOCIETY

Most of the great early civilizations were patriarchal. In early human societies men tended to hunt, fight, and venture forth, whereas women were entrusted with the care of children and the home. This situation was due in part to the fact that women, as the most obvious agents of human reproduction, were the guardians of future generations and, as such, were too precious to be placed at risk. In taking on the active business of running society outside the home, men also assumed responsibility for the influence and wealth that was generated by that society. The notion that a woman's domain was the home and only the home seemed, to some people at some times, to take on the character of a confinement.

The notion that women should not be placed at risk has endured. From ancient times until the nineteenth century, exploration was often part of a process of conquest that was undertaken by armies and involved considerable bloodshed. It seems unsurprising that there were few—if any—women in the exploring parties of, for instance,

Alexander the Great or Francisco Pizarro. A number of explorers met their death, often violently. The desire to shield women from such danger may be considered a somewhat chivalric form of prejudice.

WOMEN IN THE EARLY EXPLORATION OF AMERICA

Much early exploration was associated with mass migration, the movement of an entire community of people to a new land. History tends to remember only the male protagonists of such ventures, but it was self-evident that no migration was worth undertaking without women. The thirteenth-century *Saga of Erik the Red* and *Saga of the Greenlanders* recall how, around the year 1009, Gudridur Thorbjarnarsdottir accompanied her husband, Thorfinn Karlsefni, on a journey from Greenland to North America. Gudrid's son, Snorri Thorfinnsson, was the first child of European descent born on the American continent.

A number of women played vital roles in the opening up of western North America to settlers from the east of the continent. Sacagawea, a Shoshone woman born in 1790, accompanied the explorers Meriwether Lewis and William Clark on their 1804–1806 expedition to explore the vast Louisiana Territory. Sacagawea's presence in the party was crucial in negotiations with native peoples not only because of her skills as an interpreter but also because her presence was seen as a guarantee that Lewis and Clark were traveling with a peaceful purpose. Sacagawea is also said to have helped the explorers by acting as a guide.

Women on the Oregon Trail

*F*rom the 1840s on, thousands of settlers traveled west across the United States along the Oregon Trail, a route that ran from Independence, Missouri, to Oregon City. The route from end to end was around two thousand miles long, and the going was tough. During the journey women not only performed a range of domestic tasks, such as cooking, cleaning, and nursing duties, but also took turns at driving wagons, herding livestock, and performing guard duty.

Below **This photograph from around 1900 shows a young female settler riding across open grazing land in Oregon.**

Jessie Benton Frémont, the wife of the American trailblazer John Frémont, also played a vital role in the opening of the West. Jessie's literary skills were instrumental in writing the reports that turned her husband into an American hero, the legendary pathfinder who had opened up the states of Washington, Oregon, and California to settlers from the east.

Jessie's determination and tenacity were on occasion as important as those similar qualities in her husband. Jessie married John in 1841 in spite of her father's strong objections, and when in 1843 John Frémont received a letter urging him not to travel to the Pacific, Jessie persuaded him to ignore it and continue with his journey.

HEIRESSES

Exploration is an expensive business and in the past was generally funded by prosperous individuals. As women often lacked direct access to sources of private wealth, they found themselves excluded from exploration for financial reasons. It is thus no coincidence that many of the female explorers of the past two hundred years have been unmarried heiresses.

Left **This 1845 illustration of the remarkable traveler Lady Hester Stanhope in Arabic dress is taken from her *Memoirs*.**

c. 1009
Gudrid gives birth to the first child of European descent born in North America.

1805
Sacagawea takes part in an expedition to explore the Louisiana Territory.

1813
Hester Stanhope becomes the first European woman to cross the Syrian desert.

1869
Alexandrine-Pieternella-Françoise Tinné is murdered in Libya while traveling to the Nile River.

1894
Mary Kingsley becomes the first European to explore parts of Gabon in West Africa.

1894–1897
Isabella Bishop explores China and Korea, despite the hostility that usually greets foreign visitors to those countries.

1897–1898
Gertrude Bell makes her first trip around the world.

1908
Annie Peck Smith climbs Mount Huascarán in Peru.

1931
Louise Boyd leads a scientific exploration of the east coast of Greenland.

1932
Amelia Earheart becomes the first woman to fly solo across the Atlantic Ocean.

Hester Stanhope (1776–1839) was the daughter of Charles, the third earl Stanhope. In 1810 Hester moved to Lebanon (on the Mediterranean coast of western Asia), where she lived for over twenty years. In her search for the ancient city of Palmyra, she became the first European woman to cross the Syrian desert. An extraordinary character who refused to adhere to local customs, she commanded considerable respect and even awe among those she met.

The Englishwoman Isabella Bishop (1831–1904) also used her inheritance to fund her own journeys. When she was advised by medical experts to travel in order to lessen the symptoms of a spinal condition, she embarked on a lifelong program of exploration. Bishop visited North America, Australia, New Zealand, Hawaii, Japan, India, Tibet, China, and many more countries besides. She made her final journey, to Morocco, at the age of sixty-nine.

Below **Amelia Earhart, photographed in Washington, DC, in 1936, giving valuable advice on air safety to a Senate board meeting.**

RIS & EWING

1963
The Russian cosmonaut Valentina Tereshkova becomes the first woman in space.

1983
Sally Ride becomes the first American woman in space.

2001
At the age of twenty-four, Ellen MacArthur becomes the youngest person ever to sail single-handedly around the world.

What Happened to Amelia Earhart?

In 1932 Amelia Earhart (1897–1937) became the first woman to fly solo across the Atlantic. Five years later, on July 2, 1937, she and her navigator, Fred Noonan, vanished during an attempt to fly across the Pacific. The U.S. government spent four million dollars searching for her, and countless search parties have combed the Pacific since, but nothing has ever been found to indicate what became of her. According to one theory, she was captured by the Japanese; according to another, she is buried on an island in the Pacific. In fact, the truth is still unknown.

Right **During the 1920s Gertrude Bell played a key role in the political affairs of Iraq and made a lasting contribution to that country's cultural life when she founded the archaeological museum in Baghdad.**

Gertrude Bell (1868–1926), another Englishwoman, used her inheritance to travel to the Alps, around the world twice, and to Iraq, where she investigated the region's rich archaeological heritage and established a national museum in Baghdad. Her knowledge of the Middle East was valued extremely highly by the British government, and she won considerable political influence.

The Californian Louise Arner Boyd (1887–1972) was an intrepid adventurer who spent the huge fortune she inherited on foreign travel. During her long life, she led many expeditions to explore and photograph the Arctic and, at the age of sixty-eight, became the first woman to fly over the North Pole.

In the modern world, many explorers are sponsored by public companies and organizations, who recognize that women should have equal access to their funds. As a result, an increasing number of significant goals in the field of exploration are achieved by women.

TRAVEL WRITERS

The proceeds of travel books helped in many cases to finance a female explorer's subsequent travels. Mary Kingsley (1862–1900), who traveled extensively in West Africa at the end of the nineteenth century, collected specimens of beetles and fish for the British Museum. Her eventful travels included a trip to Gabon, where she risked encountering a tribe of cannibals. Kingsley's books about West Africa demonstrate a degree of understanding of the plight of black Africans that was not always evident among male European visitors to the continent. Freya Stark (1893–1993), another British writer, journeyed

Valentina Tereshkova *BORN 1937*

Born in the village of Maslennikovo, northeast of Moscow, at the age of twenty-six Valentina Tereshkova became the first woman in space. On June 16, 1963, Tereshkova was launched in *Vostok 6* on a journey of seventy hours and fifty minutes, during which time she made forty-eight orbits of the earth. Before the voyage the Soviet authorities did not reveal the identity of the cosmonaut on board *Vostok 6*, in case the Soviet Union was preempted by the United States in the competition to score another first in the space race. Indeed, it was not until the historic spaceflight was announced on the radio that Tereshkova's own mother knew about it. Tereshkova never returned to space again.

Below In 1942 Freya Stark was awarded the Royal Geographical Society's Founder's Medal, one of many honors she received in her lifetime.

throughout Turkey and the Middle East and published over twenty books about the people, culture, and local history of the countries she visited.

HIGH ACHIEVERS

Women broke records in a variety of fields of endeavor during the twentieth century. The American mountaineer Annie Peck Smith (1850–1935) climbed many mountains including, in 1897, the Citlaltépetl volcano in Mexico—at 18,406 feet (5,610 m), the highest peak in the Western Hemisphere that had been climbed by a woman. In 1900 she climbed the Jungfrau in Switzerland and Monte Cristallo in the Dolomites. In 1908 she became the first person to reach the 21,812-foot (6,648 m) summit of Mount Huascarán in Peru. The north peak of this mountain was named Cumbre Aña Peck in her honor.

In 1963 the Soviet cosmonaut Valentina Tereshkova became the first woman to fly into space, only two years after Yury Gagarin had become the first human to do so. It was another twenty years before Sally Ride, an American woman, matched Tereshkova's feat by flying on the *Challenger* space shuttle. In 1999, on her third shuttle flight, Eileen Collins became the first woman to be given command of a spacecraft (she led a mission aboard *Columbia*). Women's participation on space missions is now a matter of course.

Above **In 2001, after an epic solo journey around the world in a catamaran, Ellen MacArthur arrived home in London to a rapturous welcome.**

During a transatlantic race in 1999, Ellen MacArthur's sixty-foot (18 m) boat was buffeted by a hurricane. She quickly discovered that it was impossible to type accurately in such extreme weather:

Hi, 3am. Freezing, soaking, and and impossible to stand. Justgot slaughtered whildt chaanging to storm jib.. THrowm up and doen on deck, washed sideways so many times. Rightnoe trying to thype, warmer as put survival suit on, very tired . . . eyes stinging still from salt . . . virtually lifted off seat here . . . slamming is bad. Bieng on the foredeck you could be a million miles away from the cabin . . . let alone human existance . . . you need breathing apparatus to work anywhere near the bow . . .

In 1986 Ann Bancroft became the first woman to reach the North Pole on a dogsled expedition. Seven years later she turned her attention to the Antarctic and led a team of four women, traveling on skis and pulling sleds, to the South Pole.

In the twenty-first century the achievements of female explorers tend not to be singled out on the basis of sex alone. In 2001, for example, the British yachtswoman Ellen MacArthur spent three months battling against high winds, rough seas, icebergs, and freezing conditions in her catamaran *Kingfisher* to become the youngest person to sail around the world. It was her youth that earned her the headlines, not her sex.

SEE ALSO

- Astronauts • Bell, Gertrude • Bishop, Isabella Lucy
- Boyd, Louise Arner • Frémont, John • Gudrid
- Polar Exploration • Sacagawea
- Space Exploration
- Tinné, Alexandrine-Pieternella-Françoise

YOUNGHUSBAND, FRANCIS EDWARD

THE INDIAN-BORN BRITISH SOLDIER and explorer Francis Edward Younghusband (1863–1942) added considerably to geographical knowledge of central Asia. In the 1880s and 1890s Younghusband explored the Karakorum and Pamir mountain ranges, and in 1904 he led a British military expedition to Tibet. Younghusband was the first Englishman to enter Lhasa, the Tibetan capital.

EARLY EXPLORATION

Francis Edward Younghusband was born in Murree, a town in the Himalayan foothills in present-day Pakistan, to British parents. After attending boarding school in England, he returned to India to serve as an officer in the British army. The British colonial authorities, concerned that the Russian Empire was planning to expand into central Asia, encouraged Younghusband and other officers to explore the lands surrounding India and to file reports on any Russian movements.

In 1884 Younghusband made his first visit to the Himalayas when he passed from Kashmir into Afghanistan. In 1886 he explored Manchuria (a region of northeastern China) with Colonel Mark Bell. The following year he returned to India by crossing the Gobi Desert. His route took him via the Muztagh Pass, a passage through the Karakorum range at an altitude of 19,000 feet (5,791 m).

VYING WITH RUSSIA

In 1889 and 1890 Younghusband made two diplomatic expeditions to central Asia as an official of the British government. In 1891 he was sent to the Pamir Mountains (in present-day Tajikistan) to check on rumors of a Russian invasion of the region. He came across a Russian commander, Colonel Yanov, who had already claimed the area for the Russian czar. Younghusband spent the evening dining with Yanov at his camp, and the two men parted as friends.

Below **In later life Francis Younghusband was one of the world's leading experts on the geography of central Asia.**

Right **In March 1904 Younghusband and his officers posed for the camera after their victory over the poorly armed Tibetan army at Chumi Shengo.**

In 1903 the British governor-general of India, George Curzon, learned of a secret treaty between the Russians and the Chinese. The Chinese claimed ownership of the mountain kingdom of Tibet; Curzon believed that the Chinese were about to sell Tibet to the Russians. Such a deal would have brought Russian troops up to the northern border of the British Empire. Curzon wrote to the Tibetan government in Lhasa, but when his letters were returned unopened, he ordered Younghusband to lead a military expedition into Tibet and to persuade the Tibetan leaders to talk to the British.

THE TIBETAN CAMPAIGN

In December 1903 Younghusband left India with one thousand Indian troops, ten thousand porters, four hundred mules, fifty British officers, and twelve Maxim machine guns. The expedition had to make its way through freezing mountain passes at heights of over 15,200 feet (4,633 m).

On March 31, 1904, the British force met the Tibetan army at Chumi Shengo. The British gave the Tibetan commander fifteen minutes to surrender. However, even though the Tibetan general had ordered his men to lay down their weapons, fighting broke out. Within minutes, over 850 Tibetans had been killed or wounded by the British guns.

Younghusband entered the Tibetan capital, Lhasa, in triumph on August 1. Tibet's leader, the Dalai Lama, fled to Mongolia. Having become the first Englishman to enter Lhasa, Younghusband discovered that there were no Russian troops in Tibet. Furthermore, as the British had killed over three thousand

1863
Francis Edward Younghusband is born in Kashmir.

1884
Makes his first journey to the Himalayas.

1886
Visits Manchuria.

1887
Makes crossing of China and Mongolia via the Gobi Desert and over the Muztagh Pass in the Karakorum range.

1888
Travels through Burma to the upper reaches of the Mekong River.

1889–1891
Maps the Pamir and Hindu Kush ranges for the Great Trigonometrical Survey of India.

1892–1894
Explores along the Amu Darya River, in Afghanistan.

1901
Helps to found the Royal Society for Asian Affairs.

1904
Leads military expedition to Lhasa; surveys Tsangpo and Brahmaputra Rivers.

1924
Organizes British expedition to scale Mount Everest.

1936
Founds the World Congress of Faiths.

1942
Dies in England.

Tibetans, the invaders were deeply resented, and the Tibetans ignored the peace and trade treaty the British forced them to sign.

LATER LIFE

After the Tibetan campaign Younghusband lived for several years in the Himalayan region of Kashmir. A keen mountaineer, as chairman of the Mount Everest Committee he organized three unsuccessful attempts to scale Mount Everest, including the 1924 British Everest expedition that ended with the death of George Mallory and Andrew Irvine.

From 1919 to 1922, Younghusband served as president of the Royal Geographical Society in London. In later life he became deeply interested in Buddhism, and in 1936 he founded the World Congress of Faiths. He wrote several books and articles about the

geography and peoples of Asia, as well as works on mountaineering and religion.

Below **British troops march into Lhasa in August 1904.**

The Great Game

*I*n the nineteenth century the British Empire in India was separated from the Russian Empire by the unmapped lands of central Asia. The British were concerned that the Russians were planning to invade Afghanistan and Tibet, a move that would bring them to the border of British India. From the 1870s on, the British sent Francis Younghusband and other officers into central Asia to gather geographical information and to check on Russian movements. For their part, the Russians were engaged in similar campaigns. The strategic rivalry between the two powers, characterized by intrigue, espionage, and strained diplomacy, became known as "the great game."

SEE ALSO

- Hillary, Edmund
- Przhevalsky, Nikolay
- Russia
- Surveys

ZHANG QIAN

WHEN ZHANG QIAN ENTERED the Chinese capital, Chang'an, in 125 BCE, his unexpected arrival—after a thirteen-year absence—caused quite a stir. Sent out in 138 BCE on a journey far to the west and not heard of since, Zhang Qian had long been given up for dead. In fact, his journey proved to be a watershed in Chinese history. Zhang Qian is remembered as China's first great explorer; after his death, Chinese influence began to spread west to a world far beyond its borders.

TROUBLE IN THE NORTH

In the second century BCE Han dynasty China was a prosperous and powerful civilization whose success drew the envy of peoples of bordering lands. A major threat came from the warmongering Hsiung Nu, who were marauding and pillaging in the north. Emperor Wu Ti (reigned 140–87 BCE) learned that the Hsiung Nu had other enemies— namely the Yüeh-chih, a people living in Bactria, a region far to the west. The Hsiung Nu had killed the king of the Yüeh-chih and made his skull into a drinking vessel.

ZHANG QIAN THE AMBASSADOR

Zhang Qian, also known as Chang Ch'ien, was an outgoing and strong-willed court official. In 138 BCE Wu Ti asked him to go to Bactria and persuade the Yüeh-chih to unite with the Chinese against the Hsiung Nu. The mission was something of a diplomatic experiment, and with Bactria lying at such a vast distance, the risks were high.

As Zhang Qian crossed the Gobi Desert, he entered Hsiung Nu territory. He was captured and imprisoned, and though he was treated well, it was fully ten years before he managed to escape. Rather than turn for home, he con-

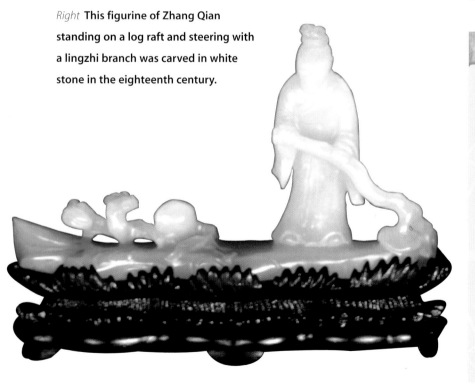

Right **This figurine of Zhang Qian standing on a log raft and steering with a lingzhi branch was carved in white stone in the eighteenth century.**

Wu Ti 156–87 BCE

Such were the achievements of the Han that all future Chinese dynasties sought to emulate them. The greatest Han emperor was Liu Ch'e, who reigned as Wu Ti from 140 BCE. Chinese society under Wu Ti was run according to the principles of order laid down by the philosopher Confucius (551–479 BCE). Wu Ti set up large-scale public building projects and greatly increased the amount of cultivated land. Agricultural innovation led to the invention of labor-saving tools and machines that were not seen in Europe for a thousand years and more.

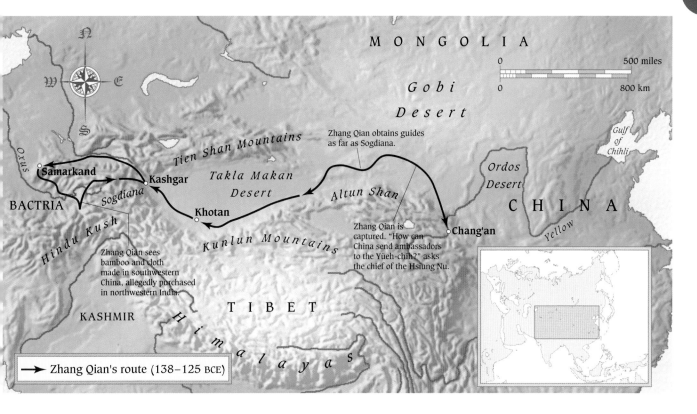

Map labels:
MONGOLIA
Gobi Desert
Tien Shan Mountains
Takla Makan Desert
Kashgar
Samarkand
Oxus
BACTRIA
Sogdiana
Khotan
Hindu Kush
Kunlun Mountains
Altun Shan
Ordos Desert
CHINA
Yellow
Gulf of Chihli
Chang'an

Zhang Qian obtains guides as far as Sogdiana.

Zhang Qian is captured. "How can China send ambassadors to the Yüeh-chih?" asks the chief of the Hsiung Nu.

Zhang Qian sees bamboo and cloth made in southwestern China, allegedly purchased in northwestern India.

KASHMIR
TIBET
Himalayas

0   500 miles
0   800 km

→ Zhang Qian's route (138–125 BCE)

Above **Zhang Qian explored routes used by traders in central Asia. As a result of his discoveries, Chinese merchants seeking to export silk to the West were able to forge a single Silk Road. Thus began the exchange of influence between China and the rest of the world.**

tinued onward and finally arrived, somewhat later than planned, in Bactria.

LIFE IN BACTRIA

Zhang Qian spent a year living among the Yüeh-chih. At such a distance from home, much was new to him. The marches of Alexander the Great had brought the influence of Greek culture to central Asia. Zhang Qian saw larger, stronger horses than those of the Chinese and unfamiliar crops, such as alfalfa and grapes.

Zhang Qian also found that Bactria was at a crossroads of trade. The Bactrians were mining lapis lazuli (a semiprecious stone) and

transporting it east to the Indus valley and west to Mesopotamia (present-day Iraq). He was amazed to find that goods from the far southwest of China had found their way into Bactrian markets.

SECOND JOURNEY

Zhang Qian returned to Chang'an in 125 BCE. Though the Yüeh-chih had refused Wu Ti's request for help against the Hsiung Nu, Zhang Qian's reports of a fledgling trade in Chinese goods greatly excited the emperor's interest. Wu Ti recognized that there was a market for Chinese produce, especially silk, in the west.

138 BCE
Zhang Qian is sent on a diplomatic mission to Bactria.

c. 137
Is captured by Hsiung Nu.

c. 127
Escapes and continues to Bactria.

125
Returns to China.

119
Explores local trade routes of central Asia.

114
Dies.

c. 100
Silk is available in the markets of Rome.

Around 119 BCE Zhang Qian went west again, with three hundred men and a large quantity of silk. Covering a swath of central Asia, he made careful notes of local trade routes. Continuing his work when he returned to Chang'an, until his death in 114 BCE, Zhang Qian set up a number of trade agreements between Han China and the peoples of central Asia.

> While in Bactria (Daxia), Zhang Qian was told that goods from southwestern Chinese kingdoms had been imported via Sind (Shendu), a land in the Indus valley.
>
> *When I was in Daxia . . . I saw bamboo canes from Qiong and cloth made in the province of Shu. When I asked the people how they had gotten such articles, they replied, "Our merchants go to buy them in the markets of Shendu." Shendu, they told me, lies . . . southeast of Daxia. . . . The region is said to be hot and damp. The inhabitants ride elephants when they go into battle. The kingdom is situated on a great river.*
>
> Ssuma Ch'ien, *Records of the Historian*

LEGACY

By 100 BCE caravans of Chinese merchants were carrying silk west along the routes forged by Zhang Qian. The Silk Road—the most important overland trade highway of the ancient and medieval world—was inaugurated. Traded across Persia as far as the borders of Europe, Chinese silk soon became a prized luxury in the Roman Empire. Indeed, by 23 CE so much Roman money was flowing east to China that Emperor Tiberius imposed a ban on the wearing of silk by men.

SEE ALSO

• Alexander the Great • Marco Polo • Silk Road
• Trade

GLOSSARY

ballast A heavy substance carried on board ships, balloons, and submersibles that improves the stability or controls the ascent and descent of a vessel.

bathyscaphe A diving vessel for deep-sea observation that is lowered by a cable from a ship.

bathysphere A spherical deep-sea observation vessel.

bearing The relationship of one point to another on the earth's surface. The bearing of point B from point A is the angle between the lines AB and AN, where N is any point due north of A.

bowsprit A long wooden post that projects forward from the front of a ship.

catamaran A ship or boat that has two hulls and is therefore difficult to capsize.

conquistador The Spanish word for "conqueror"; specifically, any of the soldiers, explorers, or settlers who, in the wake of Columbus's discovery of the Americas, helped to establish the Spanish presence in Central and South America during the sixteenth century.

Cree A member of a major group of Algonquian peoples that once inhabited a vast swath of Canada stretching from Hudson Bay west as far as the Great Slave Lake.

draft The depth that the submerged part of a vessel lies beneath the water.

feudal Referring to a system of political and social organization that prevailed in medieval Europe, according to which a commoner served a lord in return for protection and, usually, the right to farm land.

folklore The body of traditional tales, customs, and art forms preserved, often orally, among any given people.

geostationary Referring to the orbit of a satellite whose altitude and velocity are such that the satellite remains over the same point of the earth's surface as the earth spins.

gonfalonier In a medieval Italian republic, a chief magistrate.

gradient A slope, expressed as the rate of ascent or descent in relation to the distance covered.

hydrography The study of seas, lakes, and rivers, especially the charting of tides or the measurement of river flow.

isthmus A narrow bridge of land connecting two larger landmasses.

log A written record of a journey; especially, the written record of a ship's daily progress.

missionary One who works, usually in a foreign country, to spread a religious faith (especially Christianity) and to give humanitarian assistance.

Quaker A member of the Society of Friends, a Christian sect founded in England in the seventeenth century that advocates a simple form of worship with no creeds, clergy, or formal church structure.

quartz A mineral of silicon dixode that takes a variety of forms, including gemstones, sandstone, and quartz sand (used in the manufacture of glass and ceramics).

radar (an acronym for "radio detection and ranging") A piece of technology, consisting of a radio transmitter and receiver, that emits radio waves and analyzes their echoes in order to identify and locate nearby objects or geographical features.

saga An Icelandic literary form whose purpose was to praise the heroic deeds of historic or legendary figures. The sagas, originally word-of-mouth stories, were written between 1100 and 1500.

seaworthy Referring to a ship that is strong and sturdy enough to be used safely for a sea voyage.

spruce beer A concoction, made from the boiled and fermented leaves and twigs of the American spruce (a tree of the pine family), that proved particularly effective at preventing scurvy during the exploration of North America.

sundial An instrument that shows the time of day according to the shadow cast by a pointer known as a gnomon.

tidal bore A high wall of water that rushes up certain narrow rivers during exceptionally high tides.

Tuareg A member of a nomadic people native to the central and western Sahara Desert region of North Africa.

water clock An instrument that measures time by the dripping of water from one container into another.

wind vane A simple device that indicates the direction in which the wind is blowing

INDEX